$15.00

Poor Orphan Trash



Printed in the United States of America.



Publisher: Liberty Press, L. L. C.
P. O. Box 14266-
Huntsville, Alabama 35815
libertypress@knology.net

ISBN 0-9729824-0-X

First Edition
Book Design – Aneita Scott and James Holmes

# POOR ORPHAN TRASH

## ABOUT THE AUTHOR

Mildred Nelson Holmes, is a graduate of Samford University in Birmingham, Alabama. Among the many honors she received while attending college was being listed in Who's Who In American Colleges and Universities. Her postgraduate experience includes television and runway modeling, fashion show coordination and commentating, teaching motivational courses, councelling, sales, business ownership and management. She and Mr. Holmes have enjoyed a successful and happy marriage since 1961.

# ACKNOWLEDGMENT

The following people greatly influenced me to write this book.

Mr. Bill O'Reilly of FOX News cable network. Mr. O'Reilly, who has writtten several best selling books and has gained rapidly growing popularity has reported on many occasions the chaos created by irresponsible parents and the numerous problems now existing in the foster parent programs around the U. S. He has also repeatedly asked the question, "Are persons who have been abused in their childhood likely to become abusers themselves."

Mr. Newt Gingrich, former speaker of the House, United States House of Representatives. Mr. Gingrich suggested that we should stop sending welfare money to children whose parents are drug addicts. He further suggested that the children be removed from these drug abusers and placed in orphanages. Although he was greatly criticized, and even chastised by members of the news media for his position, it is my humble opinion that Mr. Gingrich has it exactly right.

# DEDICATION

Dr. Ernest Eugene Cox
October 3, 1892 – April 24, 1961
Superintendent, Baptist Children's Home
Troy, Alabama

My rescuer
whose patience and guidance was the medicine
that helped me cure my anger
and set me in the right direction.

Mr. Robert Hobson Shirey, Sr.
October 18, 1907 – November 11, 2002
Superintendent, Baptist Children's Home
Troy, Alabama

who introduced me to the joy of music, and
whose ever present humor taught me
how to enjoy life to the fullest.

# POOR ORPHAN TRASH

# ONE

We didn't know why we were brought from the cane fields that day, but we really didn't care, even if it was for punishment. It was late summer and the rattlesnakes looked for a cool place to hide. Their place of choice seemed to be at the base of the sugar cane that grew in huge clumps and, by that time of ripeness, had brown leaves that frayed and lay curled around the roots. The snakes were well hidden and hard to see, as they looked so much like the foliage.

By the time I was ten years old, I learned to smell them, poke them out with my hoe and chop off their heads. I was not a fearless child. I was terrified every second, every step, and every cane I cut. It's just that I was more afraid of my grandparents than I was of the snakes.

When we arrived at the house, my grandparents, Mama and Papa, were sitting on one side of the room. The strangest looking man I had ever seen was seated on the other side. He was short, dumpy, and the entire right side of his face had been burned to the point of heavy scarring. Even his right eyebrow was missing! His eyes were too small for his round, mottled face and the wire, rimmed glasses that he peered through gave him a stern, mean look.

I should have been frightened, but I wasn't. This was, to me, the most beautiful man I had ever seen! He was wearing a navy blue suit and a red paisley tie. I had only seen one other man so clean, and wearing a suit! He introduced himself as Mr. Cox, in a queer, rasping voice that made his words even more unbelievable. He told us children that he had heard how our grandparents were mistreating us, and that he was there to help. Before he could do anything, however, he had to confirm it with us.

The four of us huddled together like dogs, that cowered from their masters, tails tucked under their bellies, out of pure fear. I remember standing there in awe of the man himself and more importantly, what he was saying. We stood stiff and silent, so he asked us again and seemed to be staring right at me, right into my very heart.

Clutching the hole in my dress with two hands, I walked directly to him and blurted, "As soon as you leave, they will beat me for this, but I'm going to tell you anyway!" So I told him.

The words rushed from my underdeveloped eleven-year-old body like floodwater. There had been no one to tell before. No one asked, because no one cared. I told him how we were treated like slaves instead of grandchildren, how they beat us with firewood, and that we were hungry most of the time. Moreover, I told him they had sold our two-year-old brother and our four-year-old sister just a month before. Then they brought home infant twin boys to love and dote on with all their hearts. How could they love them but not their own grandchildren?

I told Mr. Cox that I did not understand any of this, but the one thing that I knew for sure, was that we needed to get away from there. I told him that my sister, Winnah, had overheard our grandmother talking about making extra money by inviting men callers to pay visits to Winnah and me. We, at our age, should not have understood what this meant, but we knew all too well. We felt that Mama would do anything for money.

Mr. Cox rose to his feet and started towards the door. Never acknowledging my grandparents, he nodded at my three siblings then looked back at me, "Be patient," he said, "I'll be back for you." "When? When?" I pressed as I ran behind him. "Take us now! Please, take us now!" "Soon," is all that came out of his mouth as he closed the car door and drove away.

I had no idea who he was or where he had come from; I just knew that we needed to go with him. I watched the shiny black car longingly as it curled around the dirt road. Soon, all I could see was dust, then nothing. This was the happiest day of my life, because somehow, I knew Mr. Cox would keep his word and come back. Meanwhile, I would just have to take my punishment for my impudence.

An extremely old tree that had been struck by lightning more than once, still stood, as if in defiance of nature's cruelty. I loved that old tree, so I walked onto her big, strong, gnarled roots that were exposed way above the soil. I sat down and leaned against her big, rough trunk as if to draw strength as I pondered my fate.

Overhead, the sound of a woodpecker caught my attention. The slight movement of raising my head to look at that old woodpecker caused him to fly away. "I wish I could fly away," I thought. "But if I did, then Mr. Cox wouldn't know where to find me," I reasoned. "What's one more beating anyway? Soon I will fly away, or drive away, with Mr. Cox," I thought, as I hummed out loud one of my favorite songs. "I'll fly away, fly away old glory, I'll fly away. When I die hallelujah bye and bye, I'll fly away." I wondered if one had to die before they could fly away. I thought about how terrific it would be just to be happy and sing happy songs.

I hugged my knees to my chest for comfort. I picked at the bark with my fingernail and thought about my life. It hadn't gotten off to a very good start.

# TWO

My very first memory was so terrifying and so senseless that I had never been able to figure it out. It was completely without understanding.

My father took my oldest sister Ruth, my little brother Harley and me, for a long walk, deep into the woods. I was at the most, three years old. I know this only because my brother Harley was two years younger than I. He was still in diapers and had yet to crawl or take his first step. When my father was drinking, he often made sarcastic remarks that when his first son was born, he was so small, he could put him into a coffee cup.

"What a man he will be," he would smirk, and then laugh. Actually, my brother was premature at birth, weighing only three pounds.

My sister Ruth, carried Harley, and Daddy carried me on his shoulders. He later put me down to let me walk. It was spring, as I remember the pleasant aroma of the trees. It seemed every step I took was like stepping onto a feather pillow, for the ground was soft and springy following a ferocious morning storm.

What started out to be an adventure soon turned into a nightmare. We had journeyed all the way to a river or large creek. I don't know which. All I remember is that our daddy told us to go down a steep bank. We were frightened and refused, so he picked up Ruth, Harley still in her arms. He carried her and Harley half way down the bank and deposited the two of them there. I was so afraid that I tried to hide, but he found me and carried me down. Slipping and sliding as he descended the steep embankment, he dropped me next to Ruth, then struggled back up the bank, disappearing from our sight.

Where he went I don't know! Why he put us in such jeopardy, I've never figured out. All I know is that the bank was slippery, wet, red clay. We tried to get out, but the harder we tried the more we slipped down.

To worsen the situation, it started to rain again, and my sister could no longer help me. It was all she could do to hold Harley with one arm and with the other, keep herself from sliding into the rushing water below. I was left to fend for myself. The rain continued; it was getting dark. The water was like a loud, black monster creeping higher and higher up the bank and coming to get us. I slid again and this time found my hands clutching a small shrub or sapling which I held on to for dear life.

I could no longer see Ruth and Harley, but I could faintly hear Ruth calling from above, "Hold on! Hold on!" Believe me, I was so tired that it would have been easy to let go and let that murky, swelling monster claim my body forever.

I don't remember how or why, but I did hold on. I held on for always, or so it seemed, until our mother found us. As impossible as it may seem, I remember practically nothing about how she got us out. I just know that she did. I suspect my sister, Winnah, who was five at the time, and who always made it her business to know everything that was going on, told my mother the direction in which we had gone.

# THREE

My mother was beautiful! Long, black, naturally curly hair and sky blue eyes, crowned her small, slim body. Her perfectly sculptured face was one that a great artist would love to have painted. She was the biggest, single most important being in the world to me. She was a smart, industrious woman whose only goal was to care for and protect her children. That objective was just about the only goal a woman, living in rural Alabama during the forties, could have. There were no jobs for women - and gracious few for men. It was a mean, hard time in history. I suppose people did the best they could.

The only form of birth control in those days was to nurse one's babies until they grew teeth. That practice, it was believed, limited pregnancies to one every two years. My mother had nine children. David, Ruth, and Talmadge were fathered by her first husband, a drunk and wife beater. My mother divorced him and married my father, who was nearly twice her age. Unfortunately, Mother went from bad to worse. In the old days, one would say, "Out of the frying pan, into the fire."

My three half siblings were, of course, born before me, so I didn't know their full story. I heard that David, as he got off a school bus one day, was hit by a car, which dragged him thirty feet. Rumor was, the accident mentally afflicted him. Mother rarely mentioned him but once did say that he could not live with us because he was sometimes violent.

Our half brother Talmadge was rumored to have been murdered by my father. I came to believe that Daddy kicked the little tot until his entrails were hanging from his body, then threw him into the pig pen for the hogs to enjoy. Of course, daddy paid no penalty for his crime. In those days, the male head of the household could treat his family anyway he chose. It was considered to be a family matter.

Our half sister, Ruth, still lived with us. Our mother was afraid that Ruth might be rushed into marriage, at age twelve. She was very beautiful and, in those days, was considered marrying age. Mother guarded her closely as she did all of her children. "Watch out for each other," she would say. "There are lots of mean, trashy folks that will hurt you, if they have half a chance."

It was mother's industry that kept us alive. Always, always except winter, there was a garden growing. We ate from the garden and everything in excess she preserved for the winter months. Of course, everyone past six years of age was expected to handle a knife. Cabbage had to be cut up to make sauerkraut. Tomatoes, okra and peppers had to be washed and sliced for canning soup. Potatoes and rutabagas would keep for a few months under the kitchen table, if left whole, clean and dry.

From our mother, we learned to scavenge good things from the wild. Blackberries, muscadines, persimmons, scallions, huckleberries, hickory nuts, and black walnuts were all there for the taking. Poke salad was there in the spring. Ugh! I hated it, but it beat being hungry.

Mother was a great planner. She squirreled away everything she could grow or find for winter. The only time I ever remember seeing her cry, was one winter when it was so cold that her canning jars, filled with the product of our hard labor, froze. The glass canning jars cracked and their contents oozed out. All the nourishment we would have had for the next few months was gone.

My mother did not cry over the wasted hours she had spent laboring and sweating to grow the vegetables; nor did she cry over the misspent hours canning those vegetables on a hot, wooden stove. She cried because she was afraid. She was terribly frightened that we would all starve to death. We very nearly did.

I remember my mother parching mule corn on the fireplace. It was actually hardened field corn, but I called it mule corn because only mules had teeth strong enough to chew it, after it had dried and hardened. After the corn was hot, our very determined mother would grind it with her own teeth, then put it into the mouths of the younger ones.

Our grandparents lived just a mile or two over the hill. They could have helped, but didn't. I don't know why. Maybe our mother was too proud to ask for help. Maybe it was because they just were not aware of our dilemma, and none of us had warm enough clothing to walk the distance to their house.

Our mother never mentioned why our father was not there to help us. There were lots of things she never mentioned. While we were desperate for the few basics that keep humans alive, she never said that we were poor. I didn't know that word. She never mentioned the word disadvantaged or poverty either.

Never, not once, did she tell us why her own family thought she was crazy, but we knew without her telling us. Our mother knew certain events would happen in advance of their occurrence. With no telephone, no television, no newspaper or magazines to inform her, she just knew. Our mother was clairvoyant.

Mother taught us many things; how to make quilts, how to make toothbrushes from sweet gum twigs, how to make brooms gathered from wild sage growing in the field. She even taught us how to make snow ice-cream, when it snowed. She also told us about God, how to treat others and endless lessons on conduct. Because of her attitude, we children developed a sense of independence and a self confidence, that comes only from knowledge that you can survive.

# FOUR

Spring came, and with it, my fifth birthday. The earth warmed, and the farmers began to plant acres of cotton and corn. Cotton was a cash crop, but corn was grown primarily as feed for the animals. One thing the two crops had in common, however, was that they both had to be weeded and thinned when the plants were about six to twelve inches tall. Weaker plants were thinned out, allowing the stronger ones to produce more abundantly. Lots of hands were needed. So, as usual, Mother, Winnah, and Ruth worked from sun up until sun down as field hands.

Any child under six years old was left on a pallet at the end of the row. I, being only five at the time, was left in charge of taking care of my brothers, Harley and Billy. Harley was three, and Billy was about nine months. I gave them water from a bottle, and frequently wiped them down with a wet rag. Mother breast fed Billy after she worked one row, then back toward us on the next row. I took my job seriously, helping my mother all I could.

All the money we made went into the company bank, which was mothers handkerchief. She carefully tied the money into the handkerchief and pinned it inside her dress with a large safety pin. We all earned the money, but our mother knew best how to spend it.

I remember Mother's spending fifty whole cents to have our mule corn ground into cornmeal. A few more cents bought soda, salt and a huge sack of flour that was packaged in a lovely, cotton print sack. Our mother saved these sacks. That's how she got the cloth to make our dresses and sunbonnets. Another thing she bought was a dozen chicks.

The chicks were so soft and cute but, mind you, they were not for entertainment. They were for feeding and protecting, until they were big enough to lay eggs. It seems that I was usually the one assigned to watching the chicks. I suppose I was selected for this chore because my older sisters had more important chores to do.

I was a dutiful five year old, but sometimes my mind wandered. One day, I lay on the ground facing the warm sun. As I lay there, I watched the white clouds move and make shapes. I was in a half sleep when I noticed a hawk circling high above. Before I could get to my feet and wave him off, that old hawk made a lightning dive making off with one of our chicks. I cried as I related the story to our mother. I felt that I had let her down, as well as the rest of the family.

A few days later, we lost another chick due to my neglect. I had been in a squabble with my sister, Winnah, but could not catch her to demonstrate my point of view. Winnah was two years older than me, nearly seven years old. She had clear, blue eyes like our mother. She also had long, straight, black hair and long legs that moved her faster than the wind. I was a fat, five year old blonde, with no speed in my dumpy legs. I was trying to figure a way to get even with Winnah, and at the same time, relieve myself of a full bladder.

I had already squatted, when a big idea came to me. I stood up, removed my under pants and headed for Winnah's favorite tree. With great effort, I climbed the tree, crawling a little way out onto a limb that was positioned directly over her favorite play area.

My bladder was getting fuller by the minute, but no sign of Winnah. Finally, after what seemed like an eternity had passed, here she came! But wouldn't you know it! Winnah decided to play on the opposite side of the tree! I dared not move to the limb above her, as I knew she would hear me and the agony of waiting so long to pee would be for naught. All I could do was wait in pain. Soon, to my great relief, she did move to the spot directly below my trap. Everything I had saved up fell in torrents all over her head and back side. "I got you! I got you!" I yelled with triumph.

My delight was short lived though, as my mother "got me" with a switch. My punishment, she explained, was not only for being mean to my sister, but also for losing another chick to that old hawk while I was up the tree.

# FIVE

How she got her hands on the ingredients I will never know, but Mother had promised Winnah a chocolate cake for her birthday. More over, she had promised seven layers -one layer for each year. Seven layers was quite a task, since, on a wood-burning stove, it is impossible to cook more than one layer at a time. So Mother started the layers several days in advance. "Um-Mm! It smelled so good!" The fragrance of cake baking in our kitchen was not an aroma we experienced very often. I actually dreamed of setting my teeth on that wonderful piece of heaven. I believed, selfishly, that Winnah's birthday meant more to me than it did to her.

Right on time, Mother had all seven layers carefully and lovingly prepared and neatly stacked. The morning of Winnah's birthday, Mother smoothed on the most yummy, mouth watering, dark brown, chocolate icing in the whole wide world. The birthday girl got to lick the spoon, while I watched her in utter admiration. I felt so fortunate that my sister had gotten born.

No sooner had Mother finished icing the cake, than a bunch of people, only some of whom I recognized, showed up at our house. Presents were certainly never expected, but they could have, at least, said "Happy Birthday" as they brushed past Winnah, on the way to the kitchen. As I watched the cake quickly disappearing, I wondered, "How did they know about it? Perhaps mother had borrowed the flour and sugar and the word had gotten out."

Being a five year old, I knew I could get away with plenty, so I maneuvered my way around skirts and legs until I got to the table. There was not a piece of cake left! Only crumbs!!! I scooped up the remnants with both hands and stuffed them in my mouth, as I ran for the door.

Good manners were important to our mother, so I knew I was in trouble again. I didn't care if I didn't have good manners; I was mad. Besides, all those big people didn't have good manners either! They ate every bit of our wonderful cake!

Just outside, I met up with Winnah who was a sight to behold. I instantly forgot my anger as I fell to the ground laughing. Winnah had taken mother's lipstick and, in protest, had painted her entire face, blood red. I didn't blame her! At least, I got some crumbs! She was the birthday girl and didn't get a taste of her own cake. I should have consoled her, but I couldn't. She stormed into the house, inviting all to see her face - a face that graphically demonstrate

d her anger. I followed behind her, still laughing. That day, I was very proud that Winnah was my sister.

# SIX

Our lives improved considerably for a while, after our father came home in early summer. Mother never mentioned where he had been, but I overheard one of our aunts say he had been in prison.

Daddy took a job in the sawmill and moved us to a better house. It was a weathered, shot gun house with a good tin roof that didn't leak. Best of all, there was a well from which we could draw water. In the past, we had to catch rainwater in big, number ten, galvanized washtubs. This was what we used for bathing and laundering clothes. Our drinking water was brought in buckets from the stream below our house. Now, we drew water directly from the well for bathing and for rinsing our clothes, after boiling them in our big black wash pot. More importantly, we no longer had to wait for rain in order to get a bath or to wash our clothes.

Mother never mentioned the word rich, but I'm certain that rich is the way I felt. We even had kerosene for our lamp, which meant we didn't have to go to bed at the moment of darkness.

Our daddy seemed to like his job and us. Every week he brought money home to our mother, and she gratefully and carefully wrapped it in her handkerchief.

This was a period of great happiness. Our mother grew a terrific garden and there was plenty to eat. There was even time to play. We had no toys but we were very innovative.

Ruth, Winnah, and I cut paper dolls from the Sears and Roebuck catalogue. We played endlessly, under a tall, shade tree. That tree soon lost its appeal, however, as a big snake crawled across the hem of Ruth's dress, slithered between my legs and kept going. Winnah said it was my fault. "That bull snake came because you were throwing a tantrum," she scolded.

Our daddy, who was arriving home from the sawmill at the time, saw the snake, and killed it with one shot. He picked it up by the tail, brought it to us, and dropped it in the middle of our paper dolls. He looked at Ruth and said, "You may as well throw that dress away; it will rot where the snake crawled on it." Sure enough, it did rot!

# SEVEN

In March of that year, I reached the ripe old age of six. Harley graduated to taking care of Billy on the pallet, and I was promoted to working up and down the rows of cotton with my mother, Ruth, and Winnah. Mother had taught me to how to chop (thin and weed) the cotton that spring. Now it was time to pick the fruit of our labor. As far as I could see was that white, fluffy stuff. It was as tall as my head. I was anxious to get started, to fill my canvass bag that fit over my shoulder with straps, and dragged after me every step I took.

Even though my mother had wrapped my hands, the very first boll of cotton I picked, brought blood. My mother instructed me not to touch the boll, just the cotton, but I just couldn't get the hang of it. By the end of the day, when the whippoorwill called, I was a bloody mess. I was so tired, nasty, and hurting that when the weighman placed my sack on the scales, I cried. I was embarrassed that my sack weighed so little. The farmers paid by the pound; and I had only a few pennies for Mother's handkerchief.

The following morning my hands were so swollen and sore, I could hardly eat my breakfast. Mother tore away the rotten part of Ruth's old dress. "No sense in this going to waste," she said, as she tore the remainder of the dress into long strips. Ruth and Winnah wrapped each other's hands, while mother wrapped mine. "I'm sorry your hands are so sore, but you know, we always do what we have to do. The man is nice enough to hire us so lets do a good job for him."

We walked to the field, arriving by sun-up. We stopped at the back-end of each row to check on Harley and Billy. We shared water, re-wet the rags around our necks, and rested briefly. Sometimes I even wet my sunbonnet to cool me down.

This day, I couldn't feel the heat. All I could think of was my throbbing fingers. Wrapping the hands did help, but it did nothing for the exposed fingers. The spikes on the bowls had made new cuts, and opened the festered ones from yesterday. Still, I was determined to do better than the day before, so I poured water on my fingers and went back to work. At the end of the day, my sack looked a little fuller, but not much. On the way to weigh in, I'm ashamed to say, I put three small rocks into my bag to make it weigh more. My pay was a few cents more, but the extra pay did not make up for the guilt I felt. I told no one of my deception; especially not my mother. She would have been horrified at my dishonesty and made me confess to the paymaster.

As the season went on, I developed a rhythm of reaching and pulling on the cotton, without touching the bolls. I still got cuts that festered and hurt for weeks, but I developed a confidence, which allowed me to pick twice as much cotton. I felt proud that I could contribute to my family, without cheating with rocks.

# EIGHT

One Saturday morning, our daddy called for all the children to come inside. I hung back, not wanting to be the first to enter. I was afraid of this man. In his deep, bellowing voice he announced, "Everybody old enough to go to school, line up over here." I got in line! Starting to school-the first grade-was the most exciting thing that I had ever thought about. Finally, I was a big kid, a soon-to-be school girl.

One at a time, Daddy had us to place our right foot on a piece of brown paper, which he outlined with a pencil. "You should have some shoes for school," he stated.

"Shoes! Wow!" I didn't remember ever having shoes before!"

It was so exciting when Daddy returned home with packages tucked under his arm! The shoes he carried were rolled up in brown paper, and when unwrapped, all looked alike, except some were larger and some were smaller. How beautiful were our brown high tops with real laces and metal hooks. As I sat in the middle of the floor getting my feet into those wonderful things, I felt a tinge of guilt for having mistrusted Daddy. The shoelaces came separately, so Mother showed us how to slip the laces through the eyelets, over the tongue, and around each hook, until each lace was finally at the top. We then received instructions in bow tying.

"Okay," my mother said, "Stand up and walk."

To my amazement, standing up was easy, but walking was a different matter. It was the strangest feeling I had ever known. I kept tripping over them. I felt like my feet were being smothered. I concluded that shoes were a great bother, so I tied them together and wore them over my shoulder most of the time. After all, they were mine to show to everyone; I just didn't want to wear them on my feet.

# NINE

The first day of school finally rolled around. I was probably the most excited first grader in the history of mankind. Moreover, I felt like a princess as I boarded the school bus. Mother had made me a beautiful, angel-wing dress from her flour sackcloth. It had tiny yellow and green flowers, trimmed in yellow-rickrack. My memory of her heating the flat irons on the stove and pressing my new dress to perfection was, to me, an example of pure love.

I felt so important and down right beautiful until I was shown to my classroom, and then my desk. I felt the cool, slick wood next to my behind and, for the first time, realized that I had forgotten to put on my panties. I froze! I reasoned that, if I was perfectly still, no one would notice. I could not think of anything, except keeping my secret. When the teacher announced, "Nap time," total mortification set in.

Needless to say, Miss Traywick and I did not get off to a very good start. She insisted that I, along with my classmates, lie down on the mat and go to sleep. I insisted that I would not lie on the mat. How could I explain that my dress might come up and show my naked behind? In the end, we both won. I did lie on the mat, even closed my eyes, pretending to sleep.

Because of my true love for learning, Miss Traywick and I started getting along really well together, until that fateful day in mid-December. I was at my desk, concentrating on my work, when someone came from behind me, kissed me on the cheek, and ran into the cloak room. I looked around the room for Randall Barnes, the boy I liked. He was nowhere to be seen.

"It was him. It was Randall," I thought with delight.

"What if it wasn't?" I wondered. So I waited and watched to see who would come out of the cloakroom. Sure enough, Randall came out, all smiling and took his seat. It was him - well, maybe! "But, what if someone else was in the cloak room?" I could not contain myself. I rose from my seat, marched to the cloakroom, and inspected it from end to end. As no one was there, I now knew for certain that Randall was the one. With great confidence, I walked back into the classroom, straight to Randall's desk. I gave him a big kiss, directly on the lips, and pranced triumphantly back to my desk.

The pride and great happiness that I felt was not shared by Miss Traywick. I got the idea that she thought I had done a great wrong, when she opened the window, broke off a large switch, and proceeded to give me a good whipping. The switching I received from Miss Traywick was nothing compared to the one my mother gave me when I got home. That tattletale Winnah told on me!!

I still didn't understand why kissing Randall was a wrong thing, but I did understand our mother's rule: "If you get a whipping at school, you get another one when you get home." She simply wanted us to be well behaved; that I truly understood.

Although reprimanded, I could not forget my love for Randall - that is - until one day, the most embarrassing day of my life, Randall destroyed all my love. Why he would do such a thing, I'll never know. Perhaps he was too timid to raise his hand and ask permission to go to the bathroom. At any rate, he must have had to pee really bad. He hid behind the classroom door and relieved himself to the cheering and laughter of all the children - all except me. I was horrified as the telltale fluid flowed into the classroom and curled around the wooden floor like a large, stealthy serpent. "Ugh!! What a sissy!" I was so embarrassed for Randall that I never spoke to him again. Not ever!

# TEN

It was just a few days before Christmas; my classmates seemed to have a growing excitement for school turning out for the holidays. Some of them talked about Santa Claus, toys and the Baby Jesus. I knew about the Baby Jesus and Santa Claus, but I had never seen evidence of either one. I had never received toys on Christmas morning, so I just stayed quiet to hide my ignorance.

I noticed a good many of the other children were quiet too. I should have been honest and admitted that I didn't expect toys. Instead, I pompously announced that I didn't need any toys; that I would rather be in school reading my books. My classmates scowled at me, but, Miss Traywick nodded her approval. I wondered if she was on to me. Perhaps! But she did allow me to take my reader home for the holidays. I wondered if Miss Traywick might be Santa Claus in disguise, as I had never received such a fine gift, or any gift, that I could remember.

That Christmas something happened that tested my firm belief in cynicism. Our daddy cut a cedar tree and stood it in the corner of the kitchen. The whole house was filled with its fragrance! I fingered the small, blue, berries, wondering what in the world was going on. Our mother furnished colored paper, which we cut into the shape of stars, bells, and fanciful things, to hang on our magical tree.

Christmas morning was totally unforgettable. As usual, being a sleepy head, I didn't want to get up. That pesky Winnah kept pulling, tugging, and urging me to get out of bed. Finally, I equated part of what she was saying, something about "Santa Claus came!"

"Came?" I asked.

"Yes! Now come on!" Winnah demanded.

Winnah was always bossing me, but she never lied to me. Nevertheless, this time, I doubted her veracity, but I did follow her to the tree.

Everyone was sitting on the floor, in a half circle, just staring. I stared too, blinking several times, to see if I was really awake or just dreaming. Our shoes were lined up at the front of the tree. Inside of our shoes, we each found an apple, an orange, and one precious nugget of peppermint candy. I made a quick decision to make my candy last a long time by limiting myself to one lick per day. I was trying to figure out how to make my apple and orange last, when mother started handing out presents.

My brothers received hand carved wooden trucks; Winnah and Ruth got the most beautiful dolls imaginable. They both had China faces and hands, with beautiful, blonde, curly hair. Oh! What long eyelashes they had that opened and closed over their blue eyes! Mother handed me my gift. As I pulled back the brown paper my heart was beating so fast I could hardly breathe, anticipating that my doll might be as beautiful as my sisters' dolls.

In one flat second, my heart stopped beating, my exaltation turned to deep depression and then anger; an anger that rose up inside of me and turned a once sweet six-year-old into an ugly monster. I was not holding a beautiful, lovable doll! No! I was holding a thing, an ugly black and white striped thing, made from a stuffed sock, with buttons sewn on for eyes, and huge, red crocheted lips! Screaming to the top of my lungs, I threw the ugly thing across the room, grabbed Winnah's beautiful doll and tore off its head. As I emptied the saw dust from the doll's body, I knew I would later regret being so mean. I did regret it too, especially when mother tore into my butt with a well-deserved switch. After that sad experience, I concluded that it was too painful and disappointing for Santa Claus to come; I wished he would just never show up again. I got my wish. He came no more!

Mother repaired the broken doll as best she could. I developed a growing shame for what I had done to Winnah's doll. We were rivals, of course, but way down deep, I really loved her.

# ELEVEN

Soon after Christmas, we were back in school, and daddy lost his job in the sawmill. He began sitting in front of the fireplace, not speaking a word, as though mesmerized by the flames. I kept wondering what he was looking at for so long. I looked into the fire, but could never see anything of real interest.

Nearly every morning our daddy would hitch the mule to the wagon and go into town in search of work. This went on for a couple of months, until one day, he came home on foot with a belly full of whiskey. In an abusive tone, he told our mother that he had sold the mule and wagon and it was none of her g_dd_mn business! Our mother knew how mean he could be in this condition so she became very quiet. We children took our cue from her and stayed quiet too. I was so afraid of him that I pulled a tablecloth over me and watched him through a small hole in the worn cloth.

As mother took the cornbread out of the oven, she tried to assure Daddy that things would get better.

"They sure as hell will," he said, "as soon as I can get rid of some of these mouths to feed and find somebody that can cook!" he shouted. "Soup and cornbread! Soup and cornbread! Can't you cook anything else?" he hollered, as he moved toward the stove. Grabbing the skillet of cornbread, he tore the bread into chunks, tossed it into the soup pot, and poured the entire contents out the back door. We went to bed hungry that night. I was already afraid of Daddy; now, I hated him.

Daddy finally got a job working in the woods. It was his job to cut timber, trim the limbs, and then snake out the logs with a mule. Each man worked with a partner, as the eight-foot cross cut saw required two men. Holding the sharp-toothed saw by its wooden handles, the men pulled back and forth in perfect unison. When a tree was cut clear through, one of the men would yell, "T-i-m-b-e-r" as it fell.

I suspect our daddy had little interest in having harmony with his assigned work partner. At home, he often cursed his very name, attacked his manhood, and bragged that he, himself, was a far better man, meaning physically stronger. I didn't doubt it!

Our daddy stood 6'4" weighing approximately 275 pounds, most of which was hard, bulging muscles. I would have thought he was handsome, had I loved him. I do not know if he was thought of as "the meanest man in the county", but I do know, he was known as the strongest. Men who wished to challenge his reputation, soon learned, that all they had to do was give daddy a few drinks of home brew and the big man lost his strength, just as Samson did in the story we learned in Sunday school.

So, it became a regular tribulation. Daddy came home every payday, mean, drunk, and with no money for mother's handkerchief. After getting him drunk, the men sometimes beat him. Without exception, they rolled him for his money. Always a willing participant, he later cried, vomited, beat us or raped Mother, with us watching. Sometimes, he just wanted to sit and listen to us sing.

Ruth had stepped on one of mother's sewing needles a year or so prior to this time. It was lodged there permanently, which gave her considerable pain. Our daddy, when he was drunk, knew how to make that needle jump right out, on it's own accord. All we children had to do was to sing to the top of our lungs, while Ruth, sitting on the floor, had to hold the bottom of her right foot level and horizontal to the rafters. The bottom of the foot had to be level to keep the three marbles from rolling off. This ritual was not an innocent game, played by a mellowed drunk. It was morbid punishment for us children, the forced participants. The object of the game, was for him to hit one of us every time the marbles rolled off, or if we quit singing. The game sometimes lasted for hours. We knew the game had mercifully ended when he passed out in this chair.

Hate for my father was increasing more and more each day. I felt like holding a gun to his temple, placing three marbles on the bottom of his foot and saying: "Now, this gun won't go off as long as the marbles are still and don't roll off."

Sometimes Daddy's drunken rampages were worse than others. On one occasion, he threatened to kill us all, so we ran into the woods where we felt safe. About midnight, we, being freezing cold, tired and hungry, decided to return to the house. Mother told us Daddy was probably asleep or passed out by now, so it might be safe to go home if we quietly slipped into bed. We came out of the woods, onto the dirt road. Still a long distance from our house, I felt a mixture of sorrow and joy. The house was on fire with an awesome blaze that grew rapidly.

"I hope he's still in there," I thought out loud.

"Don't be as mean to him as he is to you," mother cautioned, as we hurried to the house.

Upon our arrival, we found our home, along with all our few meager possessions were gone. I was amazed at how fast it had burned. I was even more amazed to find Daddy, sound asleep, snoring loudly in the front yard. That night, we too slept in the yard. At least, we derived benefit from the heat of our now smoldering house.

I'm not sure how we survived this disaster. I have a sense that our neighbors may have shared clothes, quilts, and other basic necessities. I do know that we moved into a far worse house, with no well nearby.

# TWELVE

Our mother used to say, "Nothing bad ever happens without something good coming out of it." In our present situation, I was hard pressed to believe her, until one day, when I went outside just to be alone and think. I knew that I did my best thinking in trees, so I sized them up, one at a time, to pick one for my very own. There, in the treetops, I could dream my dreams and still monitor everything that went on below.

I was just about to mount my selection, when I felt a pair of eyes staring at the back of my neck. Turning, my eyes beheld a beautiful sight - a fluffy, white puppy, complete with a wagging tail. I instantly knew he was mine.

"Come here, Snowball," I commanded!

He came right to me, wagging his fluffy tail, licking me with his long wet tongue and filling my heart with perfect joy and adulation. Love is a wonderful thing; it makes up for everything bad. I instantly loved Snowball so much that, for the first time, I was willing to defy my mother when she said I couldn't keep him. She said we didn't have enough food for us, much less a dog! My heart sank, as I knew my mother had made the correct assessment. I also knew that her word was final, no room for negotiation.

To my great surprise and disbelief my daddy spoke up, "Oh, let her keep the damn dog; he can hunt in the woods if he gets hungry."

Wow! Daddy was finally good for something! I had noticed he was trying to improve; maybe he was trying to make up for being so mean.

In the early spring, we had terrible thunderstorms to roll through our county. It seemed that before we could clean up from one, another came through. Each time, our mother was petrified. She huddled us to the center of the room and had us to put our heads down. She prayed.

While she prayed, I usually slipped away from the group to the nearest window. I wanted to see what was happening! Goodness! I didn't want to miss anything. I also wanted to be sure Snowball was okay.

Maybe it was because nothing really bad had ever happened to me during a storm, which made me love storms. Magical things seemed to happen. Huge trees bent, swayed, and danced across the sky. They moved to a rhythm of the wind; the music of the thunder, highlighted by awesome streaks of lightning, illuminating the black sky. The pageantry was addictive and good for the soul.

# THIRTEEN

As usual, we started working the fields before school was out. Some children worked all day missing their schoolwork. Mother was a great believer in learning, so we worked from five until seven, then went to school. Mother continued to work. Snowball stayed with me until school time. He was usually with mother when we got home. We joined her in the fields after school each day. Again, it was time to weed, thin, and pull the fresh smelling soil around the plants. All it took was lots of hands with willing hearts.

One thing that our worse house had was three mature peach trees. Their pink flowers were so beautiful when they blossomed. Soon they were loaded with small green peaches.

"Don't eat any until I tell you; green peaches will give you stomach aches," mother warned.

Wow! Mothers have a terrible habit of reading young minds! We tried to obey her, by not even looking at the growing peaches. But one day, they looked so big, so plump, that we could not resist. Ruth slipped into the kitchen, bringing back a couple of paring knives. We began peeling the peaches, throwing the peelings into the briers to hide the evidence from mother.

Snowball, I suppose out of curiosity, ran into the nearby brier patch. We heard him yelp just once, and then the most dreaded sound on earth came from the same location. It was the sound of a rattlesnake. I'm sure we all started yelling at once, as Snowball limped from the brier patch, staggered and fell to the ground!

Daddy came running from the house, shotgun already cocked. One shot took off the huge snake's head and gave freedom to a rabbit that the snake had apparently just started to swallow. The poor rabbit was trying to get away but daddy shot him too, putting him out of his misery. Daddy then buried the snake and the rabbit in the same hole.

In all the excitement, I did not notice that Snowball had crawled away. He had wedged himself as far under the house as he could get.

"Let him die in peace," Daddy demanded. "He just crawled up under there to die."

My heart sank into my feet. It had not occurred to me that Snowball might die. If he should die, I wanted to die right along with him.

As claustrophobic as I was of low spaces, not to mention the snakes that loved to hide under the house, I crawled toward Snowball with great haste.

"It's my fault, Snowball, it's my fault! I didn't mind mother."

Tears blinded my way as I confessed every wrong I had done during my entire life. When I finally reached him, I was surprised at how swollen he was. He hardly looked like Snowball! Just the same, I pulled and tugged until I got him and myself from under the house.

My mother was there when I came out. At the least, I expected a strong tongue-lashing. Seeing my face, I believe she thought I was being punished enough.

"Is there nothing I can do to save him?" I asked.

Mother answered, "Make a thick pallet of cottonwood leaves on the front porch. Pour water on the leaves, then place him on it. I will boil some cockle burrow leaves in milk, which you must get him to drink. Then all you can do is pray. Ask Jesus to save him," she instructed.

I did exactly as my mother told me. I tried to get him to drink. He couldn't. I sat by him and prayed every minute of the day, continuing into the night, after mother had put me to bed. The next day Snowball died; a large part of me died with him. A little dog who had never hurt anyone had died due to my disobedience.

# FOURTEEN

School was no fun anymore. Nothing was, without Snowball. So I was glad to see school come to an end. Maybe working in the fields, especially picking cotton, would give me the punishment I deserved.

As I had pledged to myself, I worked extra hard that summer, always with a heavy heart. We had a bumper crop of peaches, so mother traded some of them for apples. We made wonderful pies to eat right away. We peeled and pared the rest of the fruit for drying. A small shed with a tin roof provided the perfect place for our precious harvest. It was simple; just put the sliced fruit on the tin roof and wait for the sun to dry it. Then we wrapped it in brown paper to keep it safe until winter.

Slowly, summer turned to fall, and we were back in school. I missed Miss Traywick but I loved my new teacher, Miss Kelly. In addition to reading and arithmetic, she taught us happy songs like, "Row, row, row, your boat, gently down the stream—merrily, merrily, merrily, merrily, life is but a dream."

Daddy didn't like Winnah very much. I think it was because Winnah had a male twin. At birth, the boy died and Winnah lived. I heard Mother say that Daddy burned Winnah's birth certificate in the fireplace as he vowed, "She ain't no daughter of mine." Daddy usually ignored Winnah. On the other hand, Daddy loved me; he gave me lots of attention. When Daddy was sober I was his sweet baby girl. When he was drinking, I was the object of his rage. Often times, in the middle of the night, I awoke to another beating. Because he loved me so much, I was the one Daddy chose to grab by the hair of the head, and beat unmercifully, as my feet dangled in mid-air.

Daddy had a big rocking chair, in which he liked rocking to and fro. Often times, he would insist that I sit on his lap. I dared not incur his wrath by refusing. When he was drinking, which was most of the time now, he would touch me in ways that I hated. Mother should have been the one that I told, but I just couldn't. So I told Winnah. That sneaky, wonderful, big sister of mine said, "What if daddy couldn't sit in the chair?"

I blinked hard, not understanding. She proceeded to get a hammer, and fixed the bottom of the rocker, so that a heavy weight would cause the bottom to crash to the floor. It did just that when daddy sat down late that afternoon. Winnah and I ran around to the back of the house before we let our laughter escape to the point of screeching. It was better than we had planned! When the seat fell through, so did daddy; his behind was stuck in the rings of the chair! We heard all the curse words we had ever heard, plus a few new ones.

# FIFTEEN

I truly admired Winnah's quick thinking. Just a week before, I had stood too close to a boiling kettle and burned a large, circular spot on my left calf. It hurt! It hurt even worse when a big, old boy pushed me down as I entered the school bus. As I fell to the floor of the bus, somehow, my big blister burst and a watery, bloody, mess began to ooze from my leg. I cried, from the pain, but not for long, as I was distracted by a scary situation. Winnah jumped between that big boy and me with her mouth in high gear.

"Leave my sister alone, you bully!" she shouted!

"Yeah, what are you going to do about it, little girl?" he fired back.

Good Lord! I just knew Winnah was about to meet her maker! But she showed no fear!

Taking a step closer to him, Winnah simply stated, "You will know what I'm going to do, when I do it."

With that, the bully extended his clenched hand and said, "Hit my fist."

Winnah stood firm. "No, _cause it's too crusty!!"

The insinuation that he was nasty, ended the confrontation. To my surprise, that bully, who was three times Winnah's size, ducked his head, hid his 'crusty' fist in his pocket, and withdrew to the back of the bus. As Winnah helped me from the floor of the bus, I was not thinking of my hurt leg; I could only think of how much I admired Winnah's sharp tongue. What a talent! I wondered if one inherited this ability. Maybe I could develop a sharp tongue by the time I became a fourth grader like Winnah.

One of mothers many sisters, Aunt Lorez, also had a sharp tongue. We didn't know her very well, but occasionally she would pay us a surprise visit. One Saturday morning, she walked into our house unannounced. We were all sitting at the breakfast table. Even our daddy was there, in his birthday suit. Seeing his naked behind from the rear, she stopped, looked for a moment, then left the house. I thought perhaps she was embarrassed. Not Aunt Lorez! She was back in a flash with a long, mean switch, which she proceeded to wear out on our daddy. She was a short, stocky woman but her extreme righteous indignation seemed to completely overwhelm Daddy. He cowered, stammered and muttered some sort of apology, as she continued to draw whelps with the switch, and lash him with her tongue.

"How dare you treat these little children like this! Look at yourself," she shouted! "You don't deserve to live on this earth, you trashy, piece of shit!"

As I sat quietly in my place, I wondered if Aunt Lorez would die and go to hell for saying bad words like 'shit'. I decided she wouldn't, as she seemed pretty God-like at the moment. The comparison of the two reminded me of another Bible story, David and Goliath. Like the wrath of God, Aunt Lorez, would not let up.

By then, daddy had his overall strap over one shoulder, when Aunt Lorez asked, "What is that terrible smell in here?"

Winnah stood erect and pointed her finger at Daddy. "He piled all of our clean, ironed clothes in the corner, and then he peed on them; I think he puked on them too!" Winnah inspired great courage on my part. Without thinking, I stood to my feet. "He didn't put his breeches on, because he has to run out the door every few minutes, because of diarrhea. Whiskey is bad for him! It makes him mean and gives him the back door trots and hillside squats."

"Well," Aunt Lorez reasoned, "I guess if you are a big enough man to make this mess, you're a big enough man to get out there and start a fire under that wash pot! I'm not letting my sister clean up after your nastiness."

What power! The giant, who usually took suggestions nor directions from no one, did exactly as Aunt Lorez directed! She told us children to go out and play while she talked to mother. Winnah probably hung around to hear what they were saying. I was glad to go, an opportunity to climb my favorite tree, and reflect on all that had happened.

Daddy acted decently for a few weeks after his whipping. He even whittled Billy a wooden man, which he gave to him for Christmas. The rest of us got switches in our shoes, as we had been bad children. I didn't care. I was on to this Santa Claus thing! I knew times were hard or our mother would never have let her children think they had been bad. I did find myself wishing that we could, at least, get an apple, an orange, or a piece of peppermint.

We received something better and more permanent. Our little sister was born! At first, I loved this little blonde with all my heart. Mother named her Willette, which I thought meant Angel as I had never heard that name before. I soon came to realize that Willette, or any other name, meant the same thing - baby girl. A state of perpetual confusion took place. I had been the baby girl of the family for a long time; now, she was the baby. I felt pushed out of my place, and felt for sure, that my life would never be the same.

# SIXTEEN

A terrible winter came upon us. Freezing rain, snow, and ice caused us to huddle by the fireplace and kept the school bus from running. For days at a time, it also kept our daddy away from his job, and away from his source of whiskey. This was a blessing. He actually went into the woods behind our house, often bringing home a squirrel or a rabbit. They were pitifully small to be divided among so many, but they were mighty tasty and kept us alive.

Thank goodness for mother's homemade quilts, or we may have frozen to death. Firewood was plentiful, as we had cut it the previous fall.

"Good planning can save your life," my mother used to say.

Was she ever right!! We kept a fire going twenty-four hours a day. The fire served little purpose for most of the house, as the wind whistled through the cracks in the walls and the floorboards. We stayed near the fire, until it was safe to do otherwise.

The weather improved and so did Daddy -for awhile. He surprised us all one day when he came home with a milk cow. She wasn't much to look at, but she gave us wonderful, nourishing, milk every day. What a prize! I was beginning to feel like we were a very fortunate family.

My optimism was short lived, as Daddy began to fall into his old ways of coming home every Friday night in a drunken, sullen state, with no money. Once, mother asked him about his money. He threatened to shoot us, or slit all our throats, while we were sleeping. These were not idle threats; we knew daddy was capable of anything when he was drinking! We children were terrified; so was our mother, but the fear did not block her reasoning. Every Friday afternoon, she put the shotgun and every knife in the house in a pillowcase. She then took the pillowcase to the cotton field near our house, hiding it among the bushes.

"Best you don't know exactly where it is," she would tell us children.

Daddy usually sobered up by Monday morning. Mother habitually retrieved the pillowcase, putting the gun and knives back into their places. She tried to fool him into thinking they had never been removed, although several times, he tore the house apart looking for them. I, experiencing terrible nightmares, did not sleep very well. I knew that a man his size did not need a weapon to kill one small woman and six little children.

# SEVENTEEN

School had let out for the summer and, as usual, we children were working as field hands, right along side of our mother. One day, we saw a man staggering down the narrow dirt road that led to our house. We were at some distance, but it appeared to be Daddy! It couldn't be! This was only Thursday! He had no money to buy whisky until payday, which was Friday!

The approaching figure was much closer to the house than we were, so we dropped our hoes, jumped cotton rows and raced toward the house with one thought in mind: "Hide the gun and the knives!" We were too late!

Daddy was in the house, just a few steps ahead of us. He approached us with a butcher knife in his hand and proceeded to cut off Mother's dress from the shoulders.

Mother yelled at us, "Go outside, children!" as her dress fell to the floor.

We didn't budge. We watched in horror his enraged behavior.

"Think you're smarter than me, do you?" he said, sounding amused, as he put the knife to our mother's throat. "Well, let me show you how smart I am!" he said, as he forced her backward toward the bed.

With a clenched fist, Daddy punched mother in the stomach and threw her on the bed. He then pulled that big penis out of his overalls and put it inside Mother. He raped her and beat her in front of his own children's eyes.

We were screaming, trying to make him quit, to get off of her. I got the gun with full intentions of shooting him dead. I did a wrong thing, in that I hesitated; I was afraid I would miss him and shoot our mother! The sight of the gun at least distracted his attention; he rolled over in my direction, grabbing the barrel of the shotgun. I was not at all surprised at the ease in which he jerked it from my hand. Frankly, I was surprised that he did not shoot me on the spot. Instead, he lunged out the door toward the east side of the house. Some of us children followed him; we kept our distance though, hiding behind bushes and such, wondering what horrible thing he would do next.

Astonishingly, he placed the barrel of the shotgun between the trusting eyes of our innocent old cow and fired, before she could blink. Seeing the spray of blood and bone fragments caused my stomach to roll over. I was about to throw up, when I saw him turn, and wobble in my direction. I improved my concealment and stayed very quiet.

Meanwhile, mother had come out onto the porch; she was still in her slip. Upon seeing her, Daddy stopped, put in another shell and raised the gun in the direction of our wonderful mother. Screaming, I ran towards him, to make him stop. I heard the sound of the gun and, in my minds eye, could see my mother blown to bits! Not so! Our mother must have seen him re-loading. She jumped off the far end of the porch, running into the woods on the west side of the house. Daddy again reached into his pocket, I'm sure for another shell. I just knew I was about to be next, a splattered mess just like our cow! Daddy withdrew an empty hand from his pocket and knocked me backward, about three feet. "Thank you Jesus!" I prayed, "Maybe you do exist!" He wouldn't have hit me had he not been out of shells.

"Now, get up from there and fix me something to eat," he ordered.

Believe me, I was glad to!

After Daddy had eaten, Winnah and I had to sing for him, while poor Ruth sat on the floor, trying to do the impossible. Every time a marble rolled off the bottom of her foot, Daddy would yell and hit one of us with his big brogan shoe.

I never thought of this as real singing. It was torture, forced singing brought on by fear and fear only. Our performance seemed to last for hours, but it probably wasn't that long. Winnah was still of strong voice, but I had become hoarse and was coughing. Daddy didn't ease up on us. I also had a full bladder, but I knew not to ask to go; it would just anger him. Finally, I just spread my legs and let it pour right where I stood.

With that, Daddy said in a disgusted tone, "Just go outside. Go on!"

We gathered up Billy and Harley and got out of there. I should have peed sooner!

We headed out the front door and slipped around to the back of the house, to retrieve our baby sister, who was sleeping on the back porch. To our surprise, our inebriated father was already on the back porch when we arrived. He was throwing Willette into the air and letting her free fall to the bed. She was screaming, as any little baby would, and he was laughing as he tossed her in the air over and over again. We were afraid he would break her neck!

Ruth approached the steps.

"What do you want?" he demanded.

"We're hungry," she replied, "can we eat from the garden?"

Mother's garden was in the back of the house.

"Go ahead, eat yourselves sick," he snarled.

As he turned to go back into the house, Ruth was poised and ready. She leaped onto the porch, grabbed the still screaming baby, and was back to us in a flash. Meanwhile, Winnah grabbed Billy, into one arm, then took Harley by the hand. I had Harley's other hand as the six of us started running down the road, in the direction mother had fled earlier that day.

We thought we had outsmarted the old lush, but to our dismay and terror he came rushing after us. I knew we could not all get away, so I did a foolish thing. Turning loose of Harley's hand, I turned and ran back in the direction of danger. Thank you God! He chased me instead of the others. I ran in circles, knowing full well it would make him sick with all that liquor in him. Once, he almost caught me, but somehow, I squirmed through his legs and darted down the road again.

This was one contest I knew I could not afford to lose. As terror stricken as I was, all I could think about was Winnah. I knew that an inebriated old sot could not catch Winnah, so I pretended to be her. I was doing pretty well, too, until I tripped! "Oh, my Lord! Here I am with a giant drunk trying to kill me, and I have to land in a clump of poison ivy vines that is probably home to fifty rattlesnakes waiting to bite me!" I was so frightened that I could not get onto my feet; the more I struggled, the more I seemed to get tangled in the vines. I was a dead girl!

A shallow stream ran across the dirt road most of the year. By that time of the year, it had dried up to a trickle, but the ground was still wet. When Daddy's big feet hit that wet mud, he skidded about ten feet and lost his balance. The crash was like that of a tree being felled. He lay there face up, arms spread, and bare toes pointing to the sky.

Finally, freeing myself from the vines, I crawled around the prostrate body, keeping a safe distance just in case he was playing possum. Working my way around his arms and to the top of his head, I crouched near him and peered into his face. He was out cold. Good!

That must have been the only way God could save me, so he did! I left him lying there and went on down the road. I didn't have to find my family; they found me. I reported to my mother what had happened. She simply said, "Good!" "Let's go home now!"

We passed Daddy's inert carcass on the road; he was still lying in the same position, but now he was snoring. We knew he would be there for hours, so we all went home for a good nights sleep.

As I lay there trying to clear my mind of the unpleasant events of the day, I heard a ruckus from the direction of our pasture. It was the noise that wild animals make when fighting over food. I knew they must be devouring our old cow, so I covered my head in an attempt to keep out the horrible sounds and eventually went to sleep.

The following Monday morning, Daddy was sober again. He went to work, never mentioning anything that had happened. It was just as though nothing had happened. We knew differently. So, that's the way it was. Life was a constant battle, a challenge to survive one day at a time.

# EIGHTEEN

Soon, school started and I was finally a third grader. I felt so special! More importantly, I felt safe while I was in school. I loved to learn everything I could. I also liked to search the school grounds to see what I could find. Sometimes I found a penny or a nickel, which I turned in to my teacher. If no one claimed it within a week, it became mine. That was the school rule. It was usually claimed by its rightful owner.

One day I found a beautiful, red, half-inch rubber ball, just perfect for playing jacks. Oh, I loved to play jacks! Of course, I had neither jacks, nor a ball. I figured, though, if I had a ball, I could substitute peach seeds for the jacks! This was the greatest treasure a girl could possess. I could not turn it in to my teacher! Quickly, I slipped the ball into my pocket, knowing that it was so small, no one would ever suspect that I had it.

I didn't feel guilty right away, but the longer that little ball stayed in my pocket, the larger it seemed to get. After several hours, it was as heavy as a softball. I saw my mother's face and heard her say over and over again, "Do the right thing." So I did. At the end of the day, I reluctantly turned in the little, red ball that I so much wanted for my-self.

Each day, I knew someone was bound to claim such a treasure, but five whole days went by, and my teacher said no one had claimed it. To my surprise, she placed that perfectly round, shiny red object in my hand.

"It is yours," she said. "I'm glad you were honest enough to turn it in."

Mother was right. "It's best to do the right thing."

Now I could show off my new ball to everyone, including my mother, and my best friend, Stoolawitch. I always thought this was a weird name, but I loved playing, dancing, and singing with her, so her name made little difference. The fact that her mother was as black as the night sky, while Stoolawitch was whiter than I, also made no difference. Her mother bragged that her daddy was a white man, but I didn't care. I just knew that Stoolawitch and her family were good people. It had to be true, because our mother said so.

Mother had the opinion that there were only two kinds of people on earth. The simple deduction to this conclusion might be black and white, or male and female. Not so! Mother's view was very simple: There were good folks and there were trashy folks. Good folks were hardworking, clean, honest people, who were always glad to help their neighbors. Trashy folks were lazy, nasty and always looking for a chance to steal and do harm to others.

I always wondered why Stoolawitch could not go to school with me. When I asked mother she said, "That's just the way it is."

I hated that kind of no-answer but I knew it was the only answer I would get. So, living only half a mile apart, Stoolawitch and I were content to play jacks every chance we got.

I knew the true meaning of friendship. I also knew the true meaning of rivalry. Since the first grade, I was told by my teacher that I had the best solo voice she had ever heard. Being the show off that I was, I begged and pleaded for the opportunity to perform in the school programs, throughout the first grade year. My begging and pleading went unrewarded, but continued well into my third grade year. Still, I was never selected. Wanda Kay was chosen for all the solo parts on every occasion. I knew why, and it hurt, but I didn't hate her for it. I simply envied her.

You see, in my mind, Wanda Kay was special. She lived in a home with electricity and running water. Her home had a paved driveway on which to skate with her magnificent roller skates. The sight of that shiny, long, blonde hair swaying with her every movement certainly gave cause for a child to yearn for a pair of roller skates. But, a child can not twist and turn, sway and float on a dirt road, like the one that led to our modest home in the woods, a cabin devoid of electric power and running water. It is hard to compete with someone like Wanda Kay when all you have is Octagon soap. It is just not a fair substitute for perfumed shampoo.

The children in our house were always clean but not shiny clean. Octagon soap had a tendency to make our hair look as dry and as brittle as a used sage broom. Wanda Kay's hair, to the contrary, was always as soft and shiny as the beautifully colored ribbons she wore, that trailed down to her new store-bought dresses. She was so bright, clean and beautiful that I did not blame her, nor question the teachers decision to always choose her, over me. Deep down, however, I was determined to have my chance to shine. That time eventually came.

One afternoon, our teacher announced that school would be let out early, in order to see the President's helicopter, which was about to land on the school grounds. She also announced that one student would be selected to board the helicopter. In a rural county, where few cars and trucks existed, it is not surprising that I didn't know what a helicopter was. The minute I saw it, however, I recognized it. Although I wasn't certain who this president was, I knew he must be important.

I yearned to be recognized, so, as the strange flying machine hovered near the ground, I burst from the group of classmates and ran toward it, shouting, "Pick me! Pick me," jumping as high as I possibly could. I felt that if I shouted loud enough, and leaped high enough into the air, the men on the helicopter wouldn't notice Wanda Kay. They couldn't pick her if they couldn't see her. And, sure enough, as I approached, a small gentleman inside extended his hand to me and assisted me inside.

As I sat there next to him, I said enthusiastically, "I can sing for you."

"Please do so," he replied with a smile.

I began. "Oh beautiful for spacious skies...."

The small, smiling gentleman's name was Harry S. Truman.

That experience taught me that being good at something does not always give you an opportunity. You have to yell louder and jump higher to be noticed, and you have to be noticed before you will be granted the opportunity to show what you can do.

# NINETEEN

It was on a Saturday afternoon when I found myself alone with daddy. No one else was in the house. Realizing the situation, I quietly started for the door. Perhaps I should have run, as my tippee toe manner did not escape his attention. Daddy grabbed me and deposited me on the kitchen table.

"Hush, hush, baby girl," he whispered, as he put my legs between his to stop my kicking. He cupped my head with his huge hands as he added, "I won't hurt you; just be still."

By now I was choking as he pushed his penis further and further down my throat. I tried to fight but there was no chance of escape. I knew it and so did he. Just as I was about to give up hope, I heard a door slam. Oh! No! It was mother and Winnah! I wanted someone to stop him but not Mother; he would surely kill her!

As I feared she would do, mother yanked me from the table and held me close to her. From fear, anger, I don't know which; I could feel my mother's whole body shaking. Her small voice had a strength to it I had never heard before.

"You get out of here; leave this house and never come back."

Daddy did nothing that I expected. He quietly started for the door, then hesitated as he looked back at mother.

"Now!" she shouted.

We stood on the porch with our eyes following daddy, as he walked away, up that long winding, dirt road. The whole time we were watching Daddy, Mother and Winnah were hugging me and consoling me. When he was out of sight, mother took me into the house and poured a large pan of water.

"A little soap will make you feel better," she declared. "Someday you will understand this for what it is; your daddy is just a piece of trash. Good daddies don't act like this."

My wonderful mother and rescuer, scrubbed my face and my mouth, then gave me salt water with which to gargle.

"Now, go outside and think about this," she instructed. "I want you to decide if you're going to let his bad actions ruin your life, or if you're going to learn something worthwhile from it."

I didn't know what was worthwhile about being attacked and shamed, but I knew without a doubt that my mother was right. She was the wisest person I knew and would ever know.

I went to my favorite tree and mounted it. Mother didn't really like the fact that I was a tree climber but she seemed to understand its calming effect on my high-strung nature. Besides, I had long since lost my baby fat, which made it easier to climb. I was less apt to fall or get stuck. As I moved from branch to branch, higher and higher, I thought about my Daddy and how angry I felt. The anger caused voluminous tears to well up in my eyes and spill down my cheeks. I stopped to rest, to wipe my eyes, and clear my throat. I could hardly swallow, as my throat was hurting worse. I decided to climb no higher, but just sit where I was and enjoy the view. It was fun to watch the birds and just see what I could see.

In a short while, I saw something I didn't want to see. Far off, I could see Daddy, coming back down the road.

"He's coming back!" I yelled. "He's coming back!" I continued to holler as I scurried down the tree.

By the time I touched the ground, mother was standing on the porch. My brothers and sisters were gathering rocks. Mother made no objection to the rocks, so I helped gather them too. When Daddy arrived in the yard and approached the porch, we all threw the rocks at him as fast and as hard as we could. This time, Daddy left with his left temple bleeding. I do not know whose rock did the damage, but I hoped it was mine. I was avenged. Daddy never came back.

Our lives greatly improved after we ran him off. We all had to work just as hard, but it was such an emotional relief not having him around. Oh, my nightmares continued for a while. One night, a giant crawfish was on the end of our bed, waving his antenna and spurting blood into my face. He glowed with bright red and green flashing lights.

I awoke to my own voice screaming, "It's the devil! It's the devil! He's going to get me!"

The only reason I knew it was a dream, was that Winnah, my bedmate, was laughing at me uncontrollably. Nonetheless, I slept under a quilt during a very hot summer's night to make sure that devilish monster did not get me.

# TWENTY

Winnah was good for me. So was Stoolawitch. I helped Stoolawitch refine her skills at jack playing with the peach seeds, and she taught me how to find doodlebugs. Doodlebugs could only be found in a very dry place. She took me under her house and showed me small mounds of dirt, with indentions in the center. Next, she took a single sage straw and spat on it.

Gently slipping the straw into the indention, she said in a rhythmic voice, "Doodlebug, doodlebug, house on fire." Sometimes, to our delight, she would bring forth a tiny translucent bug on the end of the straw.

I was good for Stoolawitch too. Often times she would, through tears, tell me how she wished she knew her daddy. Each time, I told her about my daddy, and how glad I was that he was gone. We both decided we had good mothers and that was enough.

By this time our baby chicks had grown into mature chickens. Mother traded all the roosters, except one, for a new hoe, but kept the hens for laying eggs. She traded the excess eggs with a man who had a rolling store. Mother always knew when it was about time for him to come. Every two weeks or so, she sent me down to the railroad tracks to watch for him. I loved this job! I liked watching the train and wondering where it was going. From the books I had read, I conjured up wonderful places, and, in my mind's eye, pictured myself being there.

I was overwhelmed with a great happiness as I daydreamed and waited for the rolling store, a wagon pulled by a mule. Candy, picture frames and all sorts of things could be purchased from the rolling store, if you had the money. We had no money for shopping, but I still enjoyed my watch duty. At its first sight, I would run to the house to alert my mother, who would hurry down the road with her precious storehouse of eggs.

For a brief period, life was good. Our mother seemed to manage on practically nothing. The only real problem we had was late winter. We, each and every one of us, came down with a deadly flu. More than once, I saw our mother try to get out of bed. Each time, it seemed that her legs would just give away. After an exhaustive effort, she would finally make it back to bed. Ruth, Winnah and I also tried to get up, but experienced the same thing, and collapsed as mother had. Our fire, which had burned out needed to be rebuilt. We needed fluids and something nourishing, but none of us could stand long enough to provide for the others.

Lucky for us, Mrs. Johnson, Stoolewitch's mother, had noticed that no smoke was coming from our chimney. She slipped and slid over the spewed ice as she trudged to our house.

"Good Lord, have mercy," she exclaimed, as she entered the house through the unlocked door. "I knowed something was wrong, I just knowed it."

She checked us out, one at a time.

Speaking to our mother she said, "Honey, y'all ain't long for this world unless somebody does something. I guess that somebody's got to be me."

With that, she went outside to get firewood, coming back with an armload. I wondered if there were black angels; she sure looked like one to me. I determined that I would think about that more when I felt better.

After building a roaring fire, Mrs. Johnson, trudged back to her house, then back to ours. She brought a large pan of cornbread and some turnip greens. At first, we could not raise our heads to eat, so she gently spooned the nourishing pot liquor from the greens, into our mouths.

Our black angel came twice a day for a week. She kept the fire going and shared whatever food, she had. Without Mrs. Johnson's kindness, we would surely have died.

We gradually regained our strength as wintry ice turned to rain, then sunshine. We went to school, worked the fields, and on Sunday, walked to church. It was a long walk to church, so we passed the time by singing and always scavenging whatever we could find along the way. Sometimes we found an empty cigarette package; the silver foil inside would be saved for making a beautiful star. On the way home, we picked wild flowers for our kitchen table.

# TWENTY-ONE

Sunday afternoon was reserved for play. We sometimes made arbor-style playhouses in the woods or looked for June bugs. They were a type of beetle that likes to roll in dung on the ground. A funny thing happened when we tied a string to his back leg. That June bug would spread his wings and fly like crazy. He could not get away so he would fly in circles, around and around, the head of the lucky holder of the string.

We also liked to play slingshot when we were out of the view of our mother. It was a dangerous game, one that required several kids. We children would find a young sapling tree, then bend it over until the top of it could be reached by the child who was "it". At the count of three, everyone turned loose of the tree, which swished "it" through the air. The trick to staying healthy was to hold on for dear life, to never, ever turn loose before the sapling got back to its upward, calm position.

Occasionally, Sunday afternoons brought a curious kind of entertainment. Apparently, the word had gotten out that Mother no longer had a husband. Dressed in his best Sunday overalls, some strange man would just show up in our front yard. Mother would come to the porch and wait for the caller to state his case. Not one man did she ever invite to stay and sit awhile on the porch. She simply thanked him for coming, and sent him on down the road. We children were very amused. They should have known mother wouldn't want another husband; she already had plenty of children.

That was the humorous side of the situation. Actually, we knew the serious truth. It was a known fact, that a woman could not survive without a man. A man usually provided financial support and protection against the elements, as well as other men. If my mother was ever afraid of being without the protection of a man, she never voiced it, nor showed it.

# TWENTY-TWO

In the early spring, mother found us a better house that was also cheaper, she said. I cried at the thought of being over three miles from Stoolawitch but unquestionably accepted our mother's decision. She was right; the house was much larger. Now, we wouldn't all have to sleep in the same room.

We had just begun to adjust to our new surroundings when, one night, mother wakened us older ones. I awoke with mother's left hand on my mouth and her right index finger pressed to her lips. I knew we were in danger. Mother pointed to the window, then cupped her right hand to her ear, meaning that we should listen. We did! It was obvious that someone was trying to quietly open the window. Mother quickly made a plan without speaking a word. Ruth, Winnah and I were assigned, by hand signals, duties that had to be carried out in perfect unison. Mother held the slop jar, which was three quarters full and stinking. At the nod of her head, I raised the shade. Winnah and Ruth opened the window, while mother slammed the feces and urine, slop jar and all, right square into the intruder's face.

We never found out who the trespasser was, but we certainly heard him yelling and cursing as he tore out of there. The next morning we investigated the footprints and noticed he had used one of our washtubs to stand on. Referring to the tub, Mother reasoned, "He was a small man, a coward who sneaks around at night like a pole cat. Now he smells like a pole cat too, so we won't have to worry about him anymore."

As the weather warmed, we found out why we had gotten a better house, at a much cheaper price. No, I am not referring to ghosts or anything aberrational. The secrets of this house were very much alive, and from the sounds they made, they were doing well. It seems that a family of rattlesnakes lived in the storm shelter under our house. At night we could hear their rattling. At first, one would sound off, then another, and another, until the sound would crescendo into one large, numbing noise.

Some of us slept in a room directly above the storm shelter. Mother knew, as we did, that the snakes could easily get into the room through the cracks in the floor, so she moved us to the other side of the house, where we all slept in the same room. The room was less dangerous, but by no means safe. Mother kept the kerosene lamp burning all night, along with a strong warning, for us children not to put our feet on the floor without waking her first.

Once, after a really fearful night of listening to the snakes, Mother loaded the last shells we had into the double barrel shotgun. Standing well away from the storm shelter door, she fired into it, making plenty noise of her own. She knew, as did we, that one blast couldn't possibly kill so many snakes, but it gave us all an opportunity to vent our frustrations. The loud boom of the shotgun brought a round of applause from the children.

Our delight was short lived as we saw that mother was in trouble. She must have discharged both barrels at the same time, as the force of the blast had knocked her small fragile body violently backward. She was holding her right shoulder, groaning with pain. Our mother, after several weeks of extreme pain, admitted to us children, that she had done a foolish thing. She was quick to add, "but it was worth it."

# TWENTY-THREE

Soon, we moved again, away from that terrible house. Any house would have been an improvement, but we actually liked this house. Located on a paved road, right on the school bus line, it stood on a hill over looking a serene pasture. The pasture was accented by a tall mountain in the background, which seemed to change color everyday. There was a garden spot and a good well that brought forth the sweetest water I ever tasted. Once again we were safe and happy.

I still liked climbing trees, but I could sit on the bank just above the curve in the road and see everything for miles. From my perch, I could view every passerby, every animal or bird that flew over my pasture. Actually, it was not my pasture, but I claimed it just the same.

I suppose our mother must have called this epoch my jumping stage, as I loved to jump the stream that curled through the middle of the pasture. I skipped through the meadow humming or singing familiar happy songs, often making up my own songs. Always, except in winter, I brought my mother a gift of wild flowers each time I returned from my special place.

All of mother's children were smart, studious, and industrious. Winnah was now in the sixth grade. My brother, Harley, was now in the second grade, and I was loving being a big fourth grader. Ruth had made it all the way to the eleventh grade. Wow! Was she beautiful! She looked great in her band uniform. I could listen to her for hours practicing her clarinet.

I asked Ruth how she got the uniform and the instrument. She said, "Anyone past the tenth grade can get an instrument if they promise to practice and not lose it." I made a promise to myself that, as soon as I was a tenth grader, I too, would have one of those beautiful, shiny things; that I would play so beautifully, even the angels would take notice.

Because our church was now much farther away, we sometimes had church at our own house. Mother told bible stories to us. She not only explained the stories but related them to our lives. What a wise, smart person, our mother was! It was hard for most people to believe she had only gone as far as the seventh grade.

Maybe that was why she so often said to us, "Learn all that you can, for knowledge is power. It's the one thing that no one can ever take away from you."

One beautiful afternoon, I boarded the school bus, as I did every afternoon for the long drive home. I usually loved riding the bus, but today, something was amiss. Winnah and Harley were in their seats, but Ruth was missing. The driver had waited as long as he could, then asking several of the older students about Ruth. He was told that, "She had been fetched home because her mother was sick." Something didn't feel just right! Winnah and I were worried. We probably prayed for the bus to go a lot faster.

Our feelings were well founded. Three men had picked Ruth up from school. Instead of taking her home, they had taken her to the woods and brutally raped her. Two of the men, according to Ruth, were the Hathcock brothers, who were boarders at our Aunt Lorez's house. The third man, she said, was Arville Bozeman, who was married to our Aunt Marie.

Our beautiful sister, who greatly resembled our mother, was badly bruised, cut and angry. No arrests were ever made. In Fayette County, Alabama, it seemed to be a man's right to attack a young woman. After all, it was her fault for being beautiful and running loose without the protection of a father or husband.

It's no small wonder that mother promised the hand of her ruined daughter to the first man who asked. Tom was an army guy, stationed in Dallas, Texas. He was home on leave when he met Ruth, whose cuts and bruises were all healed by then. Three days later the two of them were married. I wondered if he knew she was defiled.

I missed Ruth, as we all did. I knew she was in Texas, a far-off land that just had to be a happy place. I often thought of her wedding day and how we all helped her dress; she let me shave under her arms! I was so honored that I gave her all I had - a quarter that I had found on the school playground. I had saved it for nearly a year. Maybe, if Tom wasn't good to her, she could use my quarter to get away from him.

Soon we received a letter from Ruth describing her new apartment. "What is an apartment?" I asked. Mother had to explain. Ruth's letter was mostly filled with stuff about Tom; how nice he was and how much she loved him. Wow! He sounded like a prince! It all sounded wonderful but I had my doubts. I suspected that she was just making the best of a bad situation. I could not make sense of it. She had to marry a man that she didn't even know, to distance herself from her attackers, who were also men. Since I couldn't figure it out, I decided that I would never, ever marry. It was simple; I did not know one, single man that I liked or trusted.

# TWENTY- FOUR

Our mother had not looked well lately. Her beautiful face had taken on a tired, gaunt look that I had not seen before. Moreover, I noticed that she could not work as much, needing more frequent rests. I dismissed her condition with the thought that she was probably just getting old. After all, she was thirty-four.

Another thing I thought about was the fact that our mother was pregnant again. I knew she had nothing to do with other men, and Daddy had been gone too long for it to be his, unless; unless our Daddy had come home while we were at school. This really worried me. If he had sneaked home and raped her, he could do it again. In her present condition, he might even kill her!

Those thoughts, and even worse ones, caused me to lose interest in school. Mother had to force me to go. I know I should have talked to mother, explained how I felt, but I couldn't. My tormenting need to protect her, developed into a poor attitude that kept me in trouble at school, on the school bus, and at home.

One afternoon, just prior to Mother giving birth to our youngest brother, she called us children together. She informed us that she had taken a bus to Fayette that day, while we were in school. She further informed us that she had gone to a doctor, who told her that she might have cancer. I had never heard that word, cancer, but I knew that we, as well as most folks, could ill afford the fees of doctors. The only time I had ever heard of anyone going to a doctor was if it was a death threatening illness.

None of us, except for our brother Billy, had ever been to a doctor. Billy had impetigo on his chin, and the area had become infected. His fever was so high, that mother suspected blood poisoning, She took him to Dr. Wright who treated him and, we were convinced, saved his life.

Cancer must be a serious thing. Otherwise, Mother would not have spent our money.

"Can the doctor save your life?" I asked.

"I don't know," mother replied honestly. "I have talked to your Aunt Lorez about this and we think it is wrong to let a strange man look at my body."

The doctor, of course, was a man. I certainly understood her attitude about men, but how would the doctor know what to do, if he didn't look at her? I didn't understand.

A mean depression slowly covered me in a mantle of dark sadness. I sat on my bank, gazing at my beloved pasture, never really seeing it. Often times, I sat on the side of our well, peering into it, looking for answers. Its dark, deepness held a fascination that was too private to tell about. It was as though the well was drawing me to it, whispering to me how cool, and peaceful I would be in the water, far below.

Far away seemed like a good thing, so each time I sat on the well, I sat closer and closer to the center. Sometimes, I tempted fate by dangling my legs into the well, halfway hoping the water would rush up and pull me under. Of course, that was impossible, so I considered jumping into the well. Probably the only thing that kept me from jumping was my strong fear of snakes. It was a known fact that snakes often inhabited wells.

All of my happy songs seemed to have deserted me. In their place were only sad ones. One song in particular stuck to my heart. I didn't know all the words, but it was about a little girl of Knoxville.

"She took an evening walk

About three miles from town.

I drew a stick up from the ground

I knocked that fair girl down

And all around, around me

Stood in her bloody flow

And now they're going to hang me.

A death I hate to die."

That's all the words I knew; I hummed them over and over again, not knowing, or even wondering, what the little girl of Knoxville had to do with my sick mother.

In the month of March, our brother Sam was delivered by Mama, our grandmother. Being the only midwife around, she was very experienced. Usually, birthing a baby only required one person, but our grandmother brought two of our aunts with her. She expected some difficulty, I suppose, due to mother's illness. I don't know what happened, as I went outside. Winnah hid behind the door to do her usual spying. Winnah later told me that at first, they thought Sam had a twin. It turned out to be, not a twin, but a large tumor. I didn't understand that word, tumor, but It had a bad sound to it.

After Sam was born, mother never regained her strength. The chores, taking care of the younger siblings, including baby Sam, were left to Winnah and me. I wasn't good at taking care of little ones, but Winnah seemed to have a natural talent. Mother had no milk for Sam, so Winnah thought up ways to keep him alive. Having no bottle, Winnah put sugar water into a handkerchief, then held Sam while he sucked it. Sometimes, when we had it, Winnah would half cook bacon. Not being crisp, Sam could suck on it. Once, when I was holding Sam and feeding the bacon, my attention wandered. Sam sucked the bacon down his throat, and Winnah had to pull it out. I felt terrible! He could have choked to death.

I don't remember how or why we moved from the place we all liked so much, but we did. We moved into to a smaller house, about a half mile below our grandparents' house. It could have been that it was on our grandparent's property. Since mother was unable to work in the fields, there was little money for food or rent, just what Winnah,

Harley and I could earn. Harley was only seven. Being very small for his age, he could not make much of a contribution.

One Sunday afternoon, mother called us together for another meeting. She seemed to be a little better. The haggard look had softened.

She began by saying, "Children, you know that I love you; you are all that I think about".

She continued, "Since I've been resting so much, I really feel that I am getting better. Well, it just seems to me that if I keep on resting, I will get lots better. Of course, if I don't work, we could all starve, so I have decided to apply for welfare." She paused.

Winnah asked, "What is welfare?"

"It's public assistance," mother responded.

"What is that?" I asked.

Mother nodded and briefly closed her eyes, then looked straight at me with those clear, blue eyes.

"It's charity," she stated with shame in her voice.

"You all know how I feel about that subject, but if I can get better, it won't last forever."

We sat there, in silence. I would have given anything if I could have taken back my question, if I had not pressed her, or shamed her.

So, once again, mother went to Fayette. Aunt Lorez went with her to put in the application for welfare. I knew how hard this must have been for mother. Her pride simply would not let her accept handouts. She must have been the most desperate woman on earth.

The day the welfare people came to inspect us, mother seemed anxious and worried that they might not approve us. She actually had Winnah to climb up to the rafters, above our kitchen, to hide the pitifully small amount of coffee she had saved, and used so sparingly. I could not understand why the inspectors might turn us down because of a fourth of a pound of coffee, when there was no food in the house. We did have a small garden that Winnah, Harley, and I tended.

The welfare inspectors did approve us. A check came each month for $63.20. On the one hand, I felt ashamed that we were getting charity. On the other hand, I knew mother could no longer work in the fields. Winnah and I started doing all the chores. Winnah was better at cooking and tending the children so I did more of the house cleaning and hauling water from the spring below.

Because of the snakes, mostly water moccasins, I was deathly afraid to go to the spring. I learned to watch for the snake doctors. That is the name that local folks gave the beautiful insect known as the dragon fly. It was said that "Where ever there is a snake doctor a snake is sure to be near by." Sometimes there were so many snake doctors flying around, the only place I felt safe was on the porch.

As much as I feared going to the spring, I despised baby-sitting even more. Sometimes I had to look after Billy, Willette, and Sam. I hated it! I especially hated changing diapers.

Willette, a toddler now, would make the biggest mess in her diapers, then sit down on the ground forcing that stinky do-do to squish out, all over her legs! Ugh!! I prayed for the day when she would be old enough to do her business like a normal, human being.

# TWENTY-FIVE

Thank the Lord, help soon arrived! One Saturday afternoon, Aunt Lorez came for a visit, and informed us that she was prepared to spend the night. "You girls," referring to Winnah and me, "have had an awful lot of responsibilities lately. I came to look after your mother and the other kids while you two go to a church singing," she explained.

"I have it all arranged. You will go with mama and papa." (meaning our grandparents). "Harley, you can go too, if you want to."

Before she could go further, I questioned, "Will we get to ride on his tractor?"

"Of course," she said. "You can ride in the trailer, but don't stand up," she admonished.

Quickly, Winnah, Harley and I washed and dressed in our Sunday best. A soaring spirit of expectation led us up the road to our grandparents' house. Sure enough, we rode with our legs dangling through the trailer gate, singing and talking the whole way. The ride was almost as special as the gospel music.

Those folks sure know how to make a joyful noise, so we joined right in. For a time, I forgot about my worry, that mother might die. I just wished that the singing could go on forever, but of course, it couldn't. On the way back, we laid down in the trailer. Gazing at the stars and the moon, I felt free and strong. I liked the wind tugging at my dress and kissing my face.

Far too soon, we arrived at our grandparents' house, where we experienced the most terrible sound I had ever heard. All the cows, mules and horses were at once bellowing, screeching and braying. As the headlights from the tractor shown on the cow pen fence, a large mountain lion jumped the fence and ran off in the direction of our house.

Our grandfather was yelling to the top of his lungs, "I'm going to kill that damn painter. I'll get everybody together with the dogs and we'll get'im."

In different parts of the world, these animals are called Mountain Lions, Pumas or Panthers. Where I lived they were called *Painters*.

After checking their stock, to make sure none had been harmed, our grandparents went into their house, closing the door behind them. Winnah, Harley and I were left standing in the yard.

Now, anyone in their right mind, should know that you can't stand in the yard all night, so we did the only thing we could do, we started walking home. Home was the same direction the mountain lion had gone. We made it past the mulberry tree before we heard anything suspicious. Then, we began hearing sounds that a large animal might make, as he moved through the brush. Harley and I started running.

"Run, Winnah, run!" I yelled.

"I can't," she hollered.

I forgot that we had just about cut her big toe off, the day before, when we were sawing firewood. So we three held hands, walked as fast as we could, and sang as loudly as we could. I honestly don't know if the mountain lion stalked us, or if it was just our fearful imagination. The result, however, was the same.

I have never before, or since, been so glad to set foot on a porch. Harley's right heel was bleeding profusely. He said the panther bit him. Winnah and I thought he probably cut it on a sharp rock. We must have looked pretty frightful, as mother and Aunt Lorez insisted on hearing all the details of our scary experience.

Aunt Lorez looked worried. "Why didn't Papa and Mama bring you home?"

We couldn't answer; it never occurred to us that they would drive us so we didn't ask.

"That does it." Aunt Lorez's face had changed from worried to stern.

“Inez, you and all your kids are moving in with me.”

She paused, then started to think out loud. “You know my husband has died, one of my boarders has left, and well, it’s a small house, but we will just double up.”

We did move in with Aunt Lorez. I was still very much aware that mother might die, but Aunt Lorez had such a confidence about her, that she gave me hope that everything would work out well.

We all knew that Aunt Lorez made and sold moonshine liqueur, but we didn’t care. If someone was dumb enough to buy and partake of it, that was their problem. Aunt Lorez’s husband had tuberculosis. Her home-brew whiskey provided for her, her daughter, and her husband until he died. Maybe, being a moonshiner, was not so bad as I had heard mother say.

Living with Aunt Lorez lifted much of the responsibility from Winnah’s shoulders and mine. She looked after Mother, Sam, Billy, and Willette, while the other three of us went to school everyday. Aunt Lorez felt about school the way mother did. You go!

Aunt Lorez was a very energetic, industrious person but taking care of us six children, plus our mother, plus her own daughter was quite a load for her to carry. Our mother, who was mostly bed ridden by now, was concerned enough to ask Winnah and me, “Are you helping your Aunt Lorez?” Of course the answer was yes. We knew from past experience, what had to be done to survive, and we were glad to do it. Our mother had taught us well.

I don’t know if Mother and Aunt Lorez changed their minds about a man, the doctor, seeing Mother’s body, or maybe he examined her through a blanket. At any rate, it was decided that mother should have radiation treatments. Mother was so sick and her poor stomach looked like crackling, cooked hogs skin. She never complained.

“I know it would be real easy to feel sorry for myself, but self pity will weigh you down like a rock thrown into the river. I’m trying to get better; I will not drown in my own self pity,” she said.

So Mother's radiation treatments continued. So did her use of a little, white pill, called morphine.

We had been living with Aunt Lorez only a short time when sudden change uprooted our lives again. It was on a Friday afternoon, when we arrived home from school, that we overheard a terrible argument going on between Aunt Lorez and our grandmother. Fearing to go inside, we stood on the porch and listened. The gist of the argument was that Mama, our grandmother, was demanding that we six children and Mother be moved to her house.

"She doesn't even like us; why should she want us to live with her?" I whispered to Winnah.

"Well, I don't know," Winnah mused. "It is certainly not because she loves us or our mother. Maybe it's because . . ."

Winnah's thought was interrupted by the opening of the door. Mama walked right past us, never acknowledging that we were there. She did turn once, shouting to Aunt Lorez, who was now standing in the doorway, "You have them there tomorrow."

We studied Aunt Lorez's face for comfort. There was none. She came out onto the porch. Hugging us to her, she said, "I've tried to help you, but, now I can't. Mama won't let me."

We did not want to go, so we gathered around Mother's bed for a final answer. "I know this is hard but we have to do what Mama wants. Beggars can't be choosers," she said with a sad finality.

So that was that! The next day we all moved to Mama and Papa's house.

# TWENTY-SIX

We should have been thrilled to be moving into such a fine house. Some said it was the biggest and best in the entire county, one of the few houses with electricity. It had been constructed with solid hand hewn logs, about fifteen inches thick, that had been chiseled into perfect squares, then put together with wooden pegs. The sheer density of the walls gave protection from the elements year round. Just for looks, I suppose, some type of clapboard covered the logs all around the outside of the house. The front porch was so wide, about fifty feet, that two separate sets of high steps were required to facilitate easy access. The house itself was like two huge rooms with a covered breezeway, or a dogtrot, in between. Large chimneys stood at either side of the house. It had the appearance of having been built to accommodate two separate families.

We were ushered into the right side of the house. I was overwhelmed at the sight of such a large, open, spacious area. Since there were no dividing walls, I stood at the front door taking in as much of this wonder as my young eyes could consume. I had never before seen such high, strong rafters. Some type of wood paneling covered most of the logs inside. The sitting area was around the fireplace, then a bedroom area, then at the far end was all kitchen. The kitchen walls were wall papered in a bright, cheery design that included colors like black, yellow, green, and red. I had never before seen wallpaper, nor, had I ever seen an icebox. I wondered how it worked.

In the very center of the room, one naked light bulb dangled on the end of a long wire that led to the ceiling beams above. My inquisitive nature led me to the string hanging down from the bulb. I was wondering how it got turned on, when Mama snatched me by my hair and shoved me toward Mother, scolding in a demeaning tone, "Now, you get over there and help set up your mother's bed. There won't be any lolly gagging around here. If you think I'm going to do all the work, you've got another thought coming!"

I saw my Mother cringe as the light drained from her eyes. She knew, as did I, that we were in trouble.

There was nothing to do now but try to endure our situation, so Winnah and I made a pact to work extra hard, to make sure none of us were any trouble to Mama and Papa. After all, we were used to work and never resented it. From then on, Winnah and I took care of Mother and the little ones, worked the fields, and did most of the house chores, except for the cooking which Mama did.

No matter how hard we labored, however, the treatment was the same. It was as though Mama and Papa looked for excuses to slap us, whip us, and verbally abuse us. It was not unusual for one or more of us to have wide blue marks on our legs and behinds. These marks were made by Papa's leather strap. To them, we were our crazy, sick mother's children, not their grandchildren.

It was almost a relief when night fell at the end of each day. Our two babies, Sam and Willette, were left downstairs in the big-room near Mother. The other four of us slept in the loft. Winnah, carrying a lantern, led the way up a makeshift, rickety ladder that had been hastily erected outside on the dogtrot between the two main structures. I wondered why the builder hadn't built a staircase from the interior of the house, as it was awfully inconvenient having to go outside in order to get to the loft.

I was used to climbing, so it didn't bother me. I did worry for Harley and Billy, as the ladder led to a small narrow landing. The landing was composed of a board about twelve inches in width and spanned the distance between the two main structures, which I estimate, was about ten feet. It had no handrails. Winnah went first, holding the light. The boys went next, passing her as they entered a small opening. I brought up the rear. From the ladder the narrow gangplank led us to a small room, with only one window. The one and only opening had no door with which to close out the elements or varmints. "Gracious!" I thought, (I knew mountain lions could climb); "I wondered if that painter would climb up and eat us, one at a time! "

Each night, as we entered the loft, the scurrying of the rats could be heard, driving fear and dread between us and a restful night's sleep. The loft was where our grandparents stored empty fruit jars and such. Some of the jars were broken and had particles of food left in them. These broken jars were a natural attraction for rats, mice and other vermin.

One small iron bed had been set up for the four of us, right in the middle of this mess. Winnah and I slept at the head of the bed and our brothers at the foot. Harley kicked me all night and, I'm sure, I kicked him right back. But, that was okay. Four to a bed provided warmth, better than the quilts that weighed heavy upon us. However, the quilts did provide safety from the rats.

Most nights, I fell asleep wondering if Mother would ever get well enough that we could get away from our grandparents and be happy again. This night, I did not wonder, for I knew. The chill in my heart was telling me that Mother was doomed to die. I was certain now, for Winnah had received a severe beating late that afternoon and even though Mother had witnessed Winnah's punishment, she was too weakened by her illness to object. Mother would never have allowed her child to be attacked, had she had the strength to stop it. Winnah moaned in her sleep, as I pondered the hateful episode.

Papa, a tall, wiry man had a beautiful head of gray curly hair. He seldom spoke, but when he did, he did so with great authority. He had yelled once at the dogs to quiet down. When they continued to bark, he directed Winnah to go outside, to stop their racket. I'm sure Winnah did her best to please Papa, but Papa did not see it that way. When Winnah returned, Papa snatched up a piece of firewood and hitting Winnah across the backside several times, exclaimed harshly "When I tell you to do something, I mean for you to do it! Now get back out there and don't come back `till those damn dogs are quiet."

Winnah missed supper that night, and I had finished doing the supper dishes, before the dogs became quiet. By then it was bedtime.

I usually hated doing the dishes or doing any chores indoors. Winnah seemed to know this and shouldered most of these responsibilities. Many times, I'm ashamed to admit, I would find excuses to get outside. My best excuse was that I had to go pee. When I got back from the outhouse, Winnah would have finished all the dishes.

This night, as I drifted into sleep, I determined that I would work harder. I knew that, by shirking my duties, Winnah had to do more than her share. We were all having a hard time, but Winnah, being the oldest, had it the hardest.

The very next day, I, myself, got a whipping from Papa. It was punishment for trying to ride his prize bull. At first, I thought he was angry because he feared the bull would hurt me. That was the meanest, biggest bull in the county. As it turned out, his concern was that I might harm his bull. I decided, then and there, that the best way to get along with Papa was to stay out of his way, to never confront him and to leave his animals alone!

There was one exception to this admonition. Papa didn't seem to mind my riding his old gray mare, which had been put out to pasture. She had, in the past, been a workhorse and had never been ridden. Papa might not have minded that I rode her, but I guarantee you she did! That old mare developed such a dislike for me that, if she even saw me walking across the pasture, she would chase me and do her utmost to stomp me. Actually, I didn't blame her! Every ten year old needs a challenge, and she was mine.

# TWENTY-SEVEN

It was decided, I'm sure by Mama, that Mother should be taken to Birmingham to see Oral Roberts. He was a young evangelist, who already had a reputation for healing the sick. In a borrowed, rattletrap old car, Aunt Lorez and Mama took Mother to see Mr. Roberts. In a world of pain, Mother laid on the back seat as they traveled over dusty, bumpy, dirt roads most of the way. Once there, they had to wait for hours to see this miraculous healer. Finally, Mother was carried in to Mr. Roberts, who laid hands on her and prayed for her recovery.

Then he looked at, and patting her hand, said, "If your faith is strong enough, you will be healed."

On the way home, Mama threw Mother's morphine pills out the car window saying, "You won't need these anymore! If you're truly righteous, you're cured".

By the time Mother was brought home that evening, she was in screaming pain. Mama said it was her own fault because she was not righteous, and her faith not strong enough. "NOT STRONG ENOUGH?" My Mother had more faith than anyone I knew! Could it be that her pain had been worsened by an arduous trip to see some stupid man? Oral Roberts did not know my mother. He could have taken lessons from her when it came to faith. Mother's pain was incredible. I stood by her bed and cried, "What can I do? Please tell me what to do."

Mother could not answer. She just groaned with agony. I turned to see Winnah standing in the kitchen. She motioned for me to come there. I could tell Winnah was up to something. She had that look on her face.

"Get a pan of water," she instructed. "We will cool her down and soothe her all we can to get her through the night. Early tomorrow, I'm going to do something."

"What can you do?" I wondered out loud.

"Well, our welfare check came today, and Mama wasn't here to get it, so I got it," she said, patting her skirt pocket to let me know where it was.

"I'll just have to sneak off, find someone to take me to Fayette, then talk somebody into selling me some pain pills."

"Good Lord." I thought, "Winnah was going to get killed.

Fayette was forty miles away.

"How will you get there?" I asked.

"I don't know, but I will. Now, lets take care of Mother."

It was a terrible night. I wished Mother would die so the pain would stop and Winnah wouldn't have to carry out her plan.

At first light, before Mama and Papa got up, Winnah eased out of the house. She told me later that she ran to our neighbor's house. They lived three or four miles away. Upon arrival, she begged Edie Gray Clark to drive her to Fayette. Winnah said that Edie was nine months pregnant and expecting to deliver at anytime. Just the same, she managed to get her big stomach behind the steering wheel of her old pick-up truck and get it on the road.

Once they arrived in Fayette, Winnah's next challenge was to convince a pharmacist, whom she had never before met, to actually cash the check, and then sell her morphine. How she did it, I don't know. I suspect that Winnah just kept talking until she wore the druggist down.

Winnah got back to the house about mid-morning. The first order of business was to relieve mother's pain. The pharmacist had given Winnah a syringe and needle. Winnah dissolved the morphine, filled the syringe and attempted to inject it directly into mothers arm. The first time she tried, the needle went all the way through Mother's scrawny arm and out the other side. I just about fainted. The second time Winnah tried, it was as though she had done it a million times before. Perfect!

Winnah kissed Mother on the cheek as she assured her, "You'll feel better in a little bit."

"You won't feel better, Winnah," I told her. "Mama is waiting for you in the back yard."

Winnah, already walking toward the back door said, "I know."

Winnah was the bravest twelve-year-old I had ever known. She walked straight to Mama. She stood very erect in front of Mama and defiantly said, "Go ahead! Beat me! You can't possibly hurt me more than you have hurt my mother."

Mama did beat Winnah, with a hickory stick. I felt every blow. When we talked later, Winnah was very pragmatic about her beating. "It was a trade," she said. "I traded my pain for mothers agony. It was worth it."

I was sorry that Winnah was caused pain, but I felt so good that Winnah had won over Mama. Mother was feeling better now, and there was not one thing, other than taking out her anger on Winnah, that Mama could do about it. Well, there was one thing she could do, and she did it. She took the remainder of the welfare money from Winnah.

# TWENTY-EIGHT

Mama was a short, stocky woman who, when gardening, could pee standing straight up without wetting her dress. I wondered how she could do that, but I dared not ask.

I've always liked to talk, to ask questions. Mama did not like questions, nor conversations. It was hard for me to believe she was related to my mother. Mother taught us; she criticized. Mother encouraged us; Mama demeaned us. When Mother punished us, it was to teach us. When Mama punished us, it was for control. I believe that Mama looked for reasons to slap us, so I learned to stay out of her reach. I also learned to lie, to avoid punishment, for myself and my brothers and sisters. Necessity teaches us many things.

It was five-year-old Billy's job to watch the baby chicks. Mama called them biddies. Everyday, one or more chicks came up missing. Every day, Billy got a whipping.

Harley and I begged Mama not to whip Billy. It was not his fault that her old black cat was stalking the chicks and eating them. Billy was just a little boy. He couldn't stop the cat, so Harley and I took matters into our own hands. To Mama's surprise, that cat just came up missing. I held him down on a stump so that Harley could chop off his head with an ax. We shamelessly buried him in a ditch. Billy's whippings stopped.

Mama was the only mid-wife in the county. She seemed to make good money, as evidenced by the roll of green backs, she kept rolled very tightly and pinned inside her dress.

One afternoon, when Mama was leaving on one of her calls, she told Winnah and me that we would have to milk old Beaulah. Beaulah was Mama's pet cow and usually preferred to milk her, herself. Mama forewarned us not to let Beaulah eat more that one bucket of feed or she might get colic. We obeyed. After our other chores were done, we got a clean bucket for the milk and set the allotted amount of feed before old Beaulah to keep her still.

Now, we had milked cows before; we knew how to do it. But we had never milked a cow that was determined not to give. Before we had extracted a single cup full, Beaulah had eaten all her feed and was trying to walk away. What a dilemma! We were in trouble if we didn't milk her; we were also in trouble if we gave her too much feed. Well, we gave her another bucket of feed and squeezed out another cup full. After feeding her about ten times, we finally had extracted close to a gallon of milk.

It had grown dark and we hadn't noticed that Beaulah was out of feed again. When she walked away, her right hind foot landed slap dab in the middle of our bucket of milk! We rushed back to the house to find that the milk was black with debris. What to do! What to do! Winnah was the sneaky, imaginative one, so I counted on her for a solution to escape punishment. Sure enough, she grabbed a piece of cheesecloth and we strained the milk over and over again until it looked perfectly white. Whew! Saved by Winnah's quick thinking! We poured the milk into a clean, glass, gallon jar and carefully placed it into the icebox. Now, if Beaulah didn't get sick, we were safe.

Beaulah did not get sick, but the next morning, Mama called Winnah and me to look at the milk. To our dismay, it had an inch deep of black stuff at the top of the jar. I denied knowing anything about the mystery. Lying was much safer than bearing the consequences of the truth. Finally, without proof of anything, Mama had us give the milk to the hogs.

At first, Mama kept Winnah and me both out of school. She said she needed us to work.

"You'll probably just grow up to have a passel of no-good-for-nothing kids just like your mother. Why should you need school?"

After much begging and pleading from Mother, Mama finally agreed to let us take turns. So we went to school every other day. I don't know how Winnah managed to keep up, most probably the same way I did. I know that my teacher helped me extra during recess, while my classmates were out playing. Sometimes, she helped me during lunch period too. Often times, she suggested that I go to the cafeteria with her, where I could have a free lunch. There is no way I can describe how embarrassing this was for me. So I lied again and again. Each time, I told her that I was not hungry. In a way, it was true; I wasn't hungry, I was starving! I was truly my mother's daughter. I would rather have starved to death than accept hand-outs.

Early that fall, Papa carried out his promise to hunt down the mountain lion. One crisp morning, several men and many, many dogs gathered in the yard of Papa's house. They were gone all day; and every hour that went by made my heart glad. Maybe it was because I knew Papa hated the panther so much that made me pull for that wily cat. I sincerely hoped the men wouldn't be able to find the mountain lion.

They found it alright! They located the den, which had a narrow opening, large enough for one dog at a time to pass through. One at a time the dogs entered the den opening and one at a time they fell victim to the cornered cat. Only six out of thirty-nine dogs came home that day - three of them in their master's arms. Within four days, only two dogs were still alive. I had a really hard time with this. I loved dogs but I was glad Papa could not make good his threat to kill the mountain lion. I wished that I could be like that mountain lion - wild, and free of Papa's abuse.

# TWENTY-NINE

I have no knowledge as to how it came about that we were allowed to go to the Halloween carnival, being held at the school. Perhaps it was because we were caught up on our chores. I doubt that. There's always plenty of work to do on a farm. I suspect Aunt Lorez probably badgered Mama into letting us go. The words play or fun had been erased from my vocabulary since moving in with Mama and Papa. I didn't care why we were getting to go. The important thing was that we were going.

We got all cleaned up, putting on our best clothes. Then Harley, Winnah and I walked the three or four miles to school. It didn't seem like we were walking. I was so excited! It seemed like we were floating to school.

"Hurry! Hurry!" I screamed elatedly.

We were anxious to see the sights and do all the fun things that kids do. I had found a dime months ago and was saving it for a special occasion. I was willing to turn loose of my dime only if this carnival was as much fun as I thought it would be. We were not disappointed.

When we arrived at our school, there was a long line of children and parents waiting to enter. We took our places at the end of the line as others arrived and got in the line behind us. I was impressed. As everyone in the county seemed to be there, this must be something really special. I felt lucky to have my place in line and even more so when it came my turn to enter the door. Someone handed me a papier-mâché, jack-o-lantern containing two pieces of hard candy. All the kids got one! Already thrilled by the jack-o-lantern, I was bedazzled by the bright lights and colorful decorations all over the gymnasium.

The first thing I noticed was a large, chalk-drawn design in the middle of the floor. It consisted of a circle within a circle, the two being joined by lines, which divided it into blocks. Each block had been numbered. I asked the nice lady if this was hopscotch. She said, "No, it is a cake walk." The object was to walk around and around the circle while somebody played music. When the music stopped, the participants also stopped. Then the nice lady drew a number from a hat and yelled it out. The person who happened to be standing on the number she called, would have his or her choice of the scrumptious array of cakes that were lined up on the table nearby. The nice lady said, "It costs ten cents to walk."

I was tempted to do the cakewalk right then, but I decided to look around first. What confusion! I could bob for apples for a penny or get a prize for dart throwing. My imagination went wild at the go fish booth. It only cost a penny, and every child got a prize. It was a string tied to a pole with a clothespin at the end of the string. After paying your penny, you dropped the clothespin over a card board fence. A tug on the string, by unseen hands, meant you had hooked a prize. What a temptation-and it cost only a penny!

The problem was, that if I spent a penny, then I would only have nine cents left - not enough for the cakewalk. I wondered what magical prize I could win if I paid just a penny for the ring toss. I was pretty good at throwing, but I knew I might lose. The spook house was where I almost gave in and spent my whole dime. It would have been fun to get really scared.

In the end, however, I decided on the cakewalk. I believed with all my heart that a beautiful coconut cake would make my mother smile. So I paid the nice lady my dime. I took my place on one of the squares and waited for the music to begin. It began and stopped, but to my dismay, I was not standing on the number that was called. So I walked again and again and again. Winnah tried to make me stop walking several times. Once, she pulled me away from the squares.

"You are embarrassing me!" she exclaimed.

I couldn't figure out why she would be embarrassed, so I hurried to the other side of the circle, placing my feet firmly on another square.

I walked many more times, until finally, someone called "Number 17." I looked at my feet. There it was-clear as day - number 17! I took possession of my coconut cake and was ready to head for home. I had gotten what I had come for.

On the way out the door, I found a quarter on the steps. Hallelujah! I was leaving with much more than I came with!

I was feeling like the queen of the carnival until Winnah said, "You must have marched twenty-five times to get that cake! Didn't you know that you could only march around one time for a dime?"

"No, I didn't," I responded. "Besides, the lady didn't tell me to quit, so I didn't."

Now, it was my turn to be embarrassed, but I didn't want Winnah to know. I ended it by saying, "I have a cake for Mother and that's all that counts."

I knew that wasn't so; I wondered why the nice lady let me walk so many times without paying again. Maybe she could see how important that cake was to me. I didn't know who she was, but in my heart I thanked her, as we slowly walked home.

# THIRTY

One Saturday morning, Winnah and I were on the back porch, sorting the week's laundry. Sam, Willette, and Billy were playing nearby. It was Harley's job to look after them, as he was almost eight years old, plenty old enough to baby-sit. I saw nothing, nor heard anything except the usual noises children make when they are playing.

Mama came running out the back door, down the steps hollering to the top of her lungs, "He raped her! He raped her!"

Without thinking, I ran after Mama and caught up to her just as she was relating to Papa what had happened.

"That Harley has raped Willette," she stated so firmly that it seemed like a fact.

I knew better. My tongue would not stay still.

"That's a bold face lie . . . they were in my sight the whole time and . . ." My defense of Harley was interrupted by a lick across the head that knocked me to the ground. Papa looked at me as if I were dirt under his feet.

"Don't you ever call my wife a liar! Now you get packin' before you get worse."

As I crawled backward, Papa told Mama, "Bring him to me."

Mama did so. It was like bringing an innocent lamb to the altar, having no idea of what he had done.

Papa had been pruning a diseased peach tree. When Harley arrived, Papa took him by the hand and said, "Now, tell me why you raped your sister!"

Harley, truthfully responded, "I didn't."

Papa picked up one of the limbs of the peach tree he had cut and hit Harley across the legs.

"Now tell me why you raped your sister."

"I didn't do it," Harley cried again and again.

Papa shouted at Harley over and over again, "why?" as he continued to beat him with a peach tree limb that was at least two inches in diameter. The small end of the limb had become broken and frayed when Papa grabbed one of Harley's legs. Holding him in mid air, he began to hit Harley with the big end of the limb around his shoulders and head. Harley had to have been in tremendous pain. Even his nose and ears were bleeding.

"I won't do it no more!" Harley groaned over and over until Papa dropped him to the ground and walked away towards the house.

Harley confessed in order to stop the torture, though he never knew why he took such a beating. Neither did I. He was just a little, underdeveloped boy with no capabilities for sex. He did not know the word rape, much less how to perform the act. He was at the age where he saw all cows as female and all horses as male.

Papa had beaten Harley many times, but this was the worst of all. He could not stand or sit for days. Winnah tried to doctor her brother, but about all she could do was clean the open gashes.

Roy, Mama's youngest son, and our uncle, is the one who told that whopping lie to Mama. I couldn't understand why he would want to get Harley in trouble.

At seventeen, Roy was already married to Wilma, who was about fifteen. They lived in the other part of Mama's house, the left side. We didn't see them very much. I only remember being in their side of the house just once. I remember they were eating store bought canned peaches and I begged for a slice. I had never seen store bought peaches before; they looked mouth-watering and yummy.

Roy and Wilma laughed at my begging and told me to go away or I would find myself in trouble. Naturally, I left. I couldn't help wondering how I could get into more trouble than I was already in. I knew my entire family was in great jeopardy. I literally prayed for something to happen to get us away from our grandparents.

Harley began wetting the bed, a habit which was a great discomfort to him and his bed-mates. I was really mad at him for making such a wet, smelly mess. I would have called him a sissy and demanded he stop peeing on me, except I knew he was still in terrible pain from Papa's beating. So, Winnah and I talked to him, reminding him of what would happen if mama found out. Harley really tried, but the wetting continued.

Mama soon discovered the secret that we were all trying to hide. Harley's already hurting body took another whipping. Mama would not climb the unstable ladder to the loft, but each morning she stood in the breezeway and demanded Harley toss down his pants. Each morning, they were wet. Each morning, Harley received another whipping, with increasing lashes. We just had to do something! Winnah advised Harley not to drink anything in the late afternoon. Harley obeyed but the wetting and whippings continued.

Finally, out of desperation, Harley and I conceived the perfect plan. We decided that if he were to tie a string around his penis, that it would remind him to get up and use the slop jar. This was bound to work! That night, Harley secretly tied the string and we all awoke to a dry bed. The only problem was, Harley was in agony. He literally could not pee; his little, worm size penis had blown up larger than a roasting ear. The string was so embedded that we could not see it, let alone get it loose.

Winnah was usually good at doctoring, but this time, she couldn't figure out what to do. There was nothing to do but turn Harley over to the only person in the house with medical knowledge. That was Mama. Her face was one of utter disdain as she took a sharp knife and started probing for the string. When she found it and cut it, a torrent of urine, mixed with blood, covered Mama's face and clothes. This time, I got a whipping right along with Harley. Somehow, we didn't care about this whipping. The memory of Mama being covered with bloody pee somehow made up for it.

# THIRTY- ONE

Winters in this part of the country were usually fairly mild. Even during the month of December, warm sunny days and mild night-time temperatures were not unusual. That year, however, the weather was much more harsh. One night, as usual, the four of us were in our little bed in the drafty loft. As the bone chilling wind blew through the entrance opening, which still had no door installed, I watched the light fissile of snow from the window and worried about our situation. Why I felt so responsible for solving our problem, I don't know. I usually looked to Winnah for solving problems. In talking to her, I knew she also felt trapped, with no solution. I could not think of a plan, which would work, so I decided we needed a miracle. Something just had to happen to help us.

As I lay there, I suddenly heard what sounded like angels singing, "Silent Night Holy Night." I rushed to the window to see a bunch of people, standing close together, singing the sweetest sounds on earth. They were caroling us! Winnah, Billy and Harley joined me to hear them sing. I took this as a sign that soon something good would happen; that we would get our miracle.

The next morning, I discovered that the caroling townspeople had not only sung for us, but had brought some used toys. Winnah was ecstatic that Harley, Billy, Willette, and Sam could have these toys. It affected me differently; for the first time in my life I felt poor. The delighted smiles of my little brothers and sister could not make up for the gray sadness of my heart. I wished that I could see things like Winnah, but I just couldn't. I decided that she was a better person than me, which only served to deepen my ongoing depression.

That January, just after Winnah's birthday, Mama announced that we were to move our bed downstairs to the big room. We thanked her, confessing that it was mighty cold in a loft that had no door or heat. "If you think I'm moving you for your own comfort, you're sadly mistaken. I've been having to wait on your mother at night. That's your job! From now on, you will see to her at night. If I have to get up for any reason, you will be in trouble," Mama informed us. Well, at least Mama was honest.

Mother had lost so much weight that she was just a bag of bones. Winnah and I could easily lift her, to wash her, and change her sheets. Of course, she had to be lifted as the cancer had eaten through her back, just at the waistline. She was paralyzed from the waist down, with no control of her bodily functions. We kept her clean, but the odor from the open sore on her back could not be cleaned away. It was a stench that permeated everything - even the pores of my skin. I had the sense that I would never be able to smell anything, nor taste anything again, which had not been flavored by this awful smell. I felt guilty that I became nauseous in her presence. This was the best person I would ever know and she was not long for this earth.

Winnah and I did see to Mother at night, as well as daytime. We were supposed to take turns sitting in a chair by her bed. Often times, I would go to sleep in the chair and not hear Mother. I tried to stay awake, but I just couldn't. Many times, Winnah kept me out of trouble by taking care of Mother when it was not her turn. One night, when Mother called for the bedpan, I heard her, but I suppose I was too exhausted to perform properly. I tried!

The next day Winnah told me that I had brought Mother a pillow, patting it and saying, "Here it is Mother, here is the bedpan."

I knew that Winnah and I were overworked but I just felt guilty that I didn't do my share better. Winnah was the big sister but we were supposed to have equal responsibilities and equal punishments.

Mama soon changed her mind about Winnah's and my nighttime duties. She said I was worthless help at night. Harley, Billy and I were put back into the loft. Winnah had to take care of Mother every night. Winnah confessed to me that she felt guilty, being near a warm fire, while we were in the freezing loft. But I was the guilty one. Due to my inability to wake up, and properly care for Mother, Winnah now had to sleep in a straight chair every night.

That spring Papa bought a new tractor that he called his iron horse. Soon after, he purchased a new pickup truck. We children might have been glad for him to have such fine things, except for feeling that he and Mama had spent our welfare money to get them.

None of our welfare money was ever spent on us. We were in sad need of clothes, especially Winnah and Harley who had outgrown everything. I could wear Winnah's old dresses but that left her with nothing. Billy wore Harley's old pants, but then, what was Harley to wear to school! We tried to discuss the problem with Mama, who was not at all receptive. She said that it was our fault, that we were ungrateful leeches, and that we should be grateful just to have a roof over our heads.

"If you want the best of everything, why don't you find a way to make some money!"

That was the last we heard on that subject, until one day, Winnah overheard mama talking about inviting men callers over.

"They want new dresses - let them earn them. I can cut down a couple of my old dresses just to get them started."

Winnah and I decided that we should not tell Mother that Mama was planning to turn us into prostitutes. It would kill her.

We never understood why our grandparents despised us so. They had fourteen children with many, many grandchildren. All of their children and grandchildren were loved and well received. Each time any of them came by, the reception was very noticeable. Hugs, kisses, even treats were not out of the ordinary. Sometimes, our cousins were left in Mama's care. As soon as their parents left, however, it became clear whose responsibility our cousins were.

Mama was in charge of the spoiling department but Winnah and I were in charge of any work brought on by their being there. In addition to our other chores, it was our job to see to it that our cousins had a pleasant time, and did not get hurt in any way. Moreover, if they made a mess, it was our job to clean it up. The worse part was, our cousins knew that they too, could abuse us and get away with it. They often hit Harley and Billy, but no matter how bad it hurt, Billy and Harley were not supposed to hit back. Harley could not accept this role. He got a bad whipping every time one of our cousins came.

One Friday morning, Winnah and I awoke to a wonderful surprise when Mama informed us, "You can both all go to school today." We might have asked "why" except we knew Mama didn't like questions. Also, we were so happy, that it did not occur to us that Mama had a good reason to want all of us out of the house. We should have known that she was up to something. We discovered her reason that afternoon, after school.

When we went to check on Mother, Billy was playing near Mother's bed, but Sam and Willette were nowhere to be seen.

We asked Mother, "Where are Sam and Willette?"

Mother was unable to respond. We frantically searched everywhere, looking for them! We knew something had happened to them without being told. We finally found Mama in the garden. She answered our question before we could ask it.

"Your Daddy's sister, Essie, came today. She is adopting your sister, Willette. Your daddy's brother, Aubrey, is adopting Sam. Now, that's all there is to it. I don't want to hear anymore about it."

I could see the rage and hurt rising up in Winnah and felt a building revenge for this woman like I had never known. We did not cry in front of Mama, but all three of us were out of control by the time we reached Mother's bed. Although we asked Mother over and over if she had given her permission, she never admitted that she did. She shook from her head to her toes as she cried. We all held each other for a long time.

In an effort to comfort us, Mother said, "As bad as it hurts, this might work out for the best."

Winnah and I tried to reason through this horrible thing, but couldn't. We knew for sure that if Mother had given her permission, she would have told us. We also knew that Mama had previously arranged this; that's why she let us both go to school on the same day. We also knew mama would do nothing, unless her palm was first crossed with money.

In our hearts, we felt that she had sold Sam and Willette. Our hearts ached from knowing that we might not ever see them again. As much as I hurt for myself, I hurt more for Winnah. Sam, especially was Winnah's baby. She was the only mother he had ever known. Without her, he would have died soon after birth.

# THIRTY-TWO

We children were shocked when we learned of our grandparents' decision to tear down their wonderful, old, log home. I believe their thinking was, that if the logs were milled, there would be enough lumber to build ten houses. By selling off the bulk of the lumber, they could build a fine, modern home with money to spare. Since Roy and Wilma had moved out, the plan was to tear down just the left side, then later the right side, after their new house was occupied.

After the roof and siding were removed, the workmen removed, one at a time, the numerous wooden pegs that had held the weather beaten logs together for so many years. Using crow bars and sheer strength, the men would pull out a few pegs, loosen and push the freed log to the ground, where it was hand carried to a flat bed truck to be driven to the saw mill. The sound was like thunder as the huge logs struck the ground, bounced, then came to rest.

The hammering and thunder-like sound continued for days, maybe weeks. Mother could not rest. The constant racket seemed to totally unnerve her. A person should have peace and quiet when they are dying. Mama and Papa did not see it that way. Mother's distress was not their concern. So Winnah gave Mother more morphine. Having taken it for so long, she seemed to require more and more. Six whole grams now, seemed to have little effect on her pain, nor her ability to sleep.

One Sunday morning Mama went on one of her calls, returning with twin boys. I had never heard of a midwife keeping the children that she had delivered, but there they were! Olive skin, black eyes, and so small, one could not help but fall in love with them. Mama cooed at them and held them as if they were her very own. Winnah and I were given the job of changing their diapers, bathing them and seeing after them.

I never knew how or why Mama acquired the twins. I do know that one afternoon, when the twins were about two weeks old, the sheriff came and demanded them. Mama refused in a loud verbal, deviant tone. To my wide-eyed amazement, right there on that long porch, the sheriff, along with two deputies pulled their guns on Mama. She had no choice. With tears in her eyes, she handed the twins to the deputy one at a time. I never knew where the boys came from, what circumstances that brought the sheriff, or where the twins were taken. I just knew that it was mighty peculiar that she could love them so much, but not us, her own flesh and blood.

# THIRTY-THREE

One evening, as I sat by my Mother's bed, I noticed that she seemed better than usual. I thought perhaps it was because the noise from tearing down the house had finally ended for the day.

"You are feeling better tonight aren't you?" I asked.

"Yes, I am," Mother responded in a weak voice.

"It's because I've finally made a decision. You know that I love you children; I've thought of everything I can to make your lives better. I thought if I could just stay alive, I could protect you. I was wrong. Your situation is worsening by the day and there is nothing I can do about it. I don't know what will happen to you children when I am gone, but I believe it will be something good. I've prayed for this miracle. I believe that God has heard my prayer, and I believe He will answer it when I am gone. Since I won't be here, you children will have to wait and watch for this miracle. My children are smart; you'll recognize it when it comes."

Mother paused for a long time. Looking at me intently, she said, "For your good, and mine, I need to die. You know that Dr. Wright was here this afternoon and I told him the same thing."

She was silent and so was I, horrified in knowing that she was telling the truth.

Mother spoke again, "You do know that I am going to die, don't you?"

"Yes ma'am," I answered honestly.

"Well, if I am going to die anyway, why not now?"

My throat was so tight that I could not answer.

"Come, look here in the crack in the wall."

As I walked to the other side of the bed, I noticed the arm and hand she was pointing with was smaller than mine, just bones. I peered into the crack.

"What do you see?" she asked.

"Lots of your little white pills," I answered.

Mother said, "I've been saving them, doing without them all I could. I figure there's enough there, plus what's left in the bottle . ." She choked up.

"Well, if I take them all at once, then I just won't wake up."

There was a long silence.

"I am so tired of pain, of waiting to die, of knowing my children are being mistreated. You, Mildred, are a very strong child, even stubborn. I know that you can do anything you set your mind to, so I am asking if you will help me," she pleaded.

I wanted to scream for this not to be happening. I wanted to make some sort of excuse like "I'm just a little girl; please don't ask this of me!" Instead, I faced the awful truth!

"Because I love you better than anything in this world I can't say no. Could I have until tomorrow to think about it?"

"Yes," she said, "then, we'll do it tomorrow."

Mother sighed as she closed her eyes to rest.

I did not go to sleep that night. Not a single minute did I sleep. I prayed all night long for Mother to die, without my assistance.

"God, I don't know if you're really there, but if you are, please let Mother die. I don't want to kill her. I don't want to do this terrible thing. But, I know that I will. I must do it tomorrow unless you take her tonight."

The next morning, Mother was still alive, so I went to the crib barn to freshen up and think about what I had to do. I was brushing my teeth when Winnah came to the barn and gave me the news.

"Mother just died," she said straight out.

“I’m so glad, I’m so glad,” rushed from my mouth, as I fell to my knees.

“Thank you God, thank you for taking her.”

I felt a gladness to be relieved of my impending duty. A great burden had been lifted from my small shoulders. I did not have to be the one to end her suffering. I did not cry. I never cried for our mother, because her agony was finally over. She stayed with us until we could bear losing her.

The hammering noise stopped. I suppose it was considered to be bad form to continue while a dead person was in the house. An ounce of that consideration would have been better appreciated while Mother was still alive.

Several people, mostly family I suppose, came by that day. One of the people who came was Aunt Pauline. She was very pretty. The few times I saw her, she always seemed to be very sweet and nice. This day she brought her two children with her. Terry was seven, the same age as my brother Billy. The two of them played horsy with a short rope. As usual, Terry was the rider. As always, Billy was the horse. Even at Terry’s young age, he knew the unequal status of the grandchildren. He was a grandson. Billy amounted to little more than a stray dog.

When Billy grew tired, Terry kicked him in his sides, as a rider would do his horse. Knowing not to resist, Billy just laid down on the ground. For some reason, Terry tied a knot in the rope, pulling it tighter and tighter around Billy’s neck. Choking, Billy defended himself by hitting Terry with his fist.

Papa, seeing what was happening, rushed down the steps from the porch. He snatched the rope from Billy’s neck and began lashing Billy with it.

“You will not hurt my grandson!” he shouted, as he continued to give Billy the beating of his life.

We children had learned that we had better not interfere when one of us was being punished. Just the same, Harley and I tried to get between Papa and Billy, to take some of the licks. Papa swatted us down as easily as he would shoo a fly.

Several big folks were watching. Not one adult came to Billy's rescue.

Three days later, at Mother's funeral, Billy's bruises and open gashes could be seen by all. His short pants only hid part of the damage. No one said anything.

Mother's funeral angered me beyond belief. A whole bunch of people peered into her open casket, cried, and acted like they loved her and were sorry that she was dead. They made pictures of her, I suppose, to remember her. I watched them and wondered why they had not shown these emotions while she was alive.

To make matters worse, some folks stood and started singing "Farther along, we'll understand it. Farther along, we'll understand why." I thought that they were saying "Father alone." I wondered what my father, daddy, had anything to do with anything. He was long gone away from us, and I wondered why they were singing about him.

Billy was sitting next to me. I focused on his wounded legs. An anger churned so hard inside of me that I could not cry at my own Mother's funeral. I crawled deep inside myself, mentally building a huge dam to hold back the tears. I would not let these people see me hurt.

The conduct of the people at the funeral, especially my grandparents, seemed so put on or faked that it all seemed unreal, that it was just a bad dream. The only real thing that happened was that our sister, Ruth, came home for Mother's funeral. I felt that everything would be okay, now. She would take us back to that wonderful place called Texas, where we could be happy again.

Ruth had cut her hair very short and looked so grown up. Tom, her husband, came with her. They brought each of us something new to wear to the funeral. These were the first store-bought clothes we children had ever worn. For Billy and Harley there were short pants and shirts. My outfit was a beautiful yellow sun dress with a bolero-type jacket and a white pique bodice. Winnah's dress was just like mine, except it was pink. Mother would have been proud to see her children look so nice.

Ruth was there only a couple of days. I yearned to go back to Texas with her. Ruth explained they did not have enough money for the bus fare, much less, enough money to feed us. She also confided that she was pregnant with her first child. She thought it might be a girl and planned to name her Jan.

On one hand, I felt really excited for Ruth and her soon-to-be baby. On the other hand, I felt doomed. I almost hated her. She was our last hope for getting away from our grandparents. Why couldn't she take us instead of having a baby! We were already here!

Ruth went back to Texas and we went back to the cane fields. Mama made it clear that, since Mother was gone, we four children would have more time for working in the fields.

Cotton and corn were planted every year, but cane was a crop that was only planted every three to four years. The vat and crusher had to be rented, so usually, enough syrup was made to last several years. Nothing was wasted. The foliage was stripped down to the base of the stalks with a hoe, then bundled for feeding animals during the winter months. Next the stalks were cut with a machete as a mule and wagon crept close behind. Children who were not large enough to handle a blade kept the wagon loaded. When the wagon bed was full, the cane was hauled to the work site where everything was set up and ready. First, the tops were cut from the stalks to be sold for seed. Then the stalks were put into a crusher.

As long as I live, I will remember that obedient mule, harnessed to a large boom and walking around and around in circles, powering the crusher that squeezed the sweet liquid from the stalks The juice was then carried to a huge copper vat that measured about six feet by nine feet by ten inches deep. The vat set atop three feet of large stones that housed a hot, continuous fire. One adult stirred the contents continuously to keep it from sticking to the bottom and sides of the vat. Several men usually stayed up all night keeping the fire going, stirring the mixture, passing a few bottles, and telling tall tales. As the water boiled from the juice, a thick sweet sorghum syrup was left to store in shiny, tin cans.

# THIRTY-FOUR

We had just begun the cane harvest when that strange looking man, Mr. Cox, made his initial visit to my grandparents' house.

Needless to say, Mama and Papa were very unhappy about my informing Mr. Cox of their terrible treatment of us. As I waited under that gnarled old tree for my punishment, the first eleven years of my life had passed before me.

Somehow, the abuse and deprivation, now, didn't matter for I knew, as our mother did, that her death would effect a change for her children.

In my heart, I felt that Mr. Cox was the person that would bring about this change. The reason I was so willing to trust him, a total stranger, was because I knew he was the miracle that Mother had prayed for.

Mama called me to come into the house. I was not at all surprised to see Papa with his leather strap wound tightly around his right wrist, waiting for me.

I assumed the expected position by leaning over the straight chair standing in front of Papa. He was ready for me. I was ready for him too.

I had decided not to cry no matter how much it hurt. I had learned that my body could be impervious to pain if I concentrated on something else.

When I did not cry out, Papa hit me harder. I felt no pain; it was blocked out by the vision of my mother's face. When the assault on me had ended, Papa commanded, "Now get on back to the cane field and earn your keep."

The next few days were filled with mixed emotions. Doubts of the existence of Mr. Cox ran across my mind as I said to myself, "Maybe

I was just dreaming. Maybe this Mr. Cox is not real." Then day-dreams of being removed from this harsh existence would replace my feelings of doubt and restore my optimism.

At last, my hope was rekindled when my brothers, my sister and I were suddenly relieved from our labor, before quitting time, and were summoned together at the house.

As we approached the front yard, my heart sang "I'll Fly Away" as I could see in the distance, a shiny black car parked under my favorite old tree. Standing beside the car was Mr. Cox. With him was a lady, very tall and very pretty. She glowed with a radiant cleanness. She wore a crisp, white blouse that was tucked neatly under her circular, printed skirt. I had never imagined such beautiful shoes! They were wedged sandals of red, yellow and green, showing of her painted toenails. I wondered how she got her hair to be so shiny and curly! My admiring thoughts were interrupted as Mr. Cox introduced the pretty lady.

"This is Miss Betty Coons," he stated. "She is from the Welfare Department."

Without thinking I spoke up. "It won't do any good for you to give us more welfare money; Mama will just take it, and won't spend any on us."

"Oh, no," Mr. Cox responded. "She's here to assist me. Before we can take you away from here, we have to make sure you're healthy. Now, Miss Coons, I want you to explain to the children what is going to happen."

Miss Coons, in a soft, confident voice suggested we sit on the steps to the porch. I found myself fingering her beautiful skirt as she informed us that . . .

"The Welfare Department has decided that you children should be placed in an orphanage called The Alabama Baptist Children's Home." She hesitated then asked, "What do you think of that?"

Winnah answered in a very grown up fashion, "That would be best."

Harley asked, "What is an orphanage?"

Miss Coons smiled, "That's a place where lots of children live; you'll have lots of playmates."

I could not contain myself, "If Mr. Cox is going to be there, I'm ready to go right now!"

Miss Coons smiled even bigger, "Oh, he will be there all right, he's the Superintendent! But you can't go there until you're checked out by a doctor."

Harley eyed Miss Coons suspiciously as he stated, "We don't need a doctor; we're not sick!"

Miss Coons very patiently reasoned, "Well, it is my job to make sure you won't get sick."

Unaware that our four lives were about to improve significantly and forever, we watched with reverence as Mr. Cox drove away, leaving with us again the promise that he would see us soon. This time was different, however, as he had left someone to protect us. From that day we would never go to the cane fields again; We would never receive another vicious beating; nor would we witness the tearing down of the remainder of the log house.

The following day Miss Coons drove us to a doctor in Fayette. The doctor poked and examined, gave us several shots each and put some kind of patch on our arms. He said something about checking us for tuberculosis, malnutrition, and some words I had never heard before. Wow, this orphanage must be some more special place if we had to do all this just to get in!

After seeing the doctor, I have a vague remembrance of Miss Coons taking us to see a man who was sitting at this real high desk. I believe he must have been a judge who made decisions for children who were not of legal age. I could decide for myself. I wanted to be with Mr. Cox. I probably told the judge that too.

It seemed like forever, but I'm sure it was just a day or so, when

Miss Coons came to see us the last time. She announced that the doctor had declared us to be healthy and that it was time to go.

"Right now?" I asked.

"As soon as you can get ready," she replied, as she handed each of us a brown paper sack in which to pack our meager belongings.

We scrubbed our faces, put on the clothes we had worn to Mother's funeral, and were out the door in minutes. Halfway down the steps, I remembered I had forgotten my seven bobby pins. As I rushed back to get them, I bumped into Mama. She glared at me as I jumped aside. I considered saying a nasty good-bye but dismissed the idea immediately. She wasn't worth it.

I got my bobby pins, floated down the steps and took my place on the back seat of the car, next to my brothers. Winnah was seated up front with Miss Coons. As Miss Coons started the engine, I felt our miracle had finally come. I was so happy that I started singing right out loud, "I'll fly away."

Miss Coons drove about five miles before stopping the car. She said our aunt, one of Daddy's sisters, wanted to say "good-bye." We didn't know this aunt very well but she had always been nice to us, the little time we were around her. She hugged us, gave us cookies and told us she wished we had a better daddy. Her son, S. L., gave us each a five-dollar bill. I had never seen a five-dollar bill before. It couldn't have meant more had it been a million dollars. I felt that we were very fortunate children as we again took our seats, trusting the rest of our lives with Miss Coons.

Soon, the dirt roads were behind us; we were traveling very fast on a black paved road with white lines down the center. I thought the white lines marked the way so Miss Coons wouldn't get lost. I began watching the lines closely wondering where they would take us. It had been so wonderful getting away from our grandparents, that I actually had not thought of the possibility of being unhappy where we were going. What if it was a worse place?

I felt numb with fear. Not knowing anything else I could do, I decided to watch the road and the white lines more intently. That way, if things were really bad, I could run away and find my way back home by following the lines. Of course, I would not live with my grandparents. I would live with my friend Stoolawich and her mother, Mrs. Johnson. It would be okay. If anyone wanted to know, I could just say my daddy was white. Everything would be okay.

The rush of wind from the open windows felt good, even exciting, like an adventure was happening. Still, I was so hot that I soon removed my bolero jacket, placing it carefully above my head on the shelf-like space under the rear window.

I tried to hear what Winnah and Miss Coons were saying but their words were carried away by the rushing air of the open windows. I could hear Winnah crying most of the time.

Soon, the rushing air, the hum of the engine, the heat of the day carried me away to a place of haunting, scary nightmares. I must have been asleep for two or three hours when I awoke with an aching neck and in a cold sweat. My beautiful dress was all wet, as was my hair. I wanted to look nice for Mr. Cox. I looked to my left. My brothers were sleeping and sweating like horses! Miss Coons was still following the white lines. She and Winnah were still talking.

Just as I was pulling myself from the clutches of sleep, our tree-lined road suddenly turned into an extremely high bridge that seemed to go on forever. Boats dotted the water far below. Fascinated by the beauty, I decided to roll the window down a little more for a better view. I had turned the knob only a little when a rush of wind grabbed my jacket and carried it right out the window. I felt like crying over my loss but would not, as I had no tears to shed. They had been walled up and collected by a dam so strong that it would never crack.

Soon, we stopped to go to the bathroom and eat the sandwiches that Miss Coons had made for us. She even bought us a cold drink. I remember mine was a big orange.

Back on the road, I found myself dozing again. I didn't want to sleep. I wanted to think about where I was going. Nonetheless, I fell into a deep sleep and was aware of nothing until the car slowed. I could hear Winnah and Miss Coons talking. Winnah had stopped crying and sounded so excited, that I raised up to see what it was all about. The car was barely moving as we drove up a long driveway, around a circle, then stopping in front of a huge building adorned by large, white columns.

Getting out of the car, Miss Coons said, "This is the administration building." Pointing to the right, she stated, "This is the boys side of the campus, and over there is the girls side," pointing to her left.

It was definitely the biggest yard I had ever seen, filled with acres of green grass that grew all the way from the street up to the side walks that stretched from one building to another.

"What a great place to skate," I thought.

Winnah, standing and looking all around was the first to speak. "I believe I'm going to like it," she said with such conviction that I thought it must be true for all of us.

# THIRTY-FIVE

We were taken into the administration building, where Mr. Cox was waiting for us. I was so glad to see him that I wanted to hug him. Of course, I didn't. I just said hello and waited to see what would happen. What happened frightened and upset me.

From the administration building we were led to one of the houses and told, "Now this will be Billy's cottage." He was left there and we proceeded to the next house. "This will be Harley's cottage." We left Harley there (at least their cottages were close together). We walked way across to the other side of the campus where I was shown to my cottage and introduced to my matron. Winnah left with our guide, to be shown to her cottage across the street.

As I watched her walk away, I felt like screaming, "Wait a minute! Something is wrong! We're not supposed to be separated! I want to be with Winnah and Harley and Billy!"

As Winnah left, I felt that she was deserting me. Surely, if she were to object, they would let her stay with me. That old feeling of wanting to jump into the well came over me.

When Miss Jesse, my downstairs matron, spoke to me, I stood silent with a blank face. When she showed me around, I equated little of what she was saying. Then she turned me over to the upstairs matron, Miss Evelyn, who had such a lyrical voice, I couldn't help but tune into what she was saying. First, she took me to the bathroom; there were four showers and three toilets. I had never seen in-door plumbing before, so she obligingly showed me how they worked.

Next, she took me to a very large bedroom. There were twelve beds more like the size of cots. Six were lined up on one side of the room and six on the other side. Between each bed was a small metal table with one drawer.

Miss Evelyn led me to the third bed against the wall, "This will be your bed and this will be your table." I started to sit down but was quickly corrected, "Beds are not to sit on; they are for sleeping."

Next, she showed me the central storage room where everyone's clothes were kept together. There was another bedroom that looked exactly like mine, twelve beds all lined up. Miss Evelyn took me back downstairs, opened the door and suggested I go out and play. I obeyed.

Just outside the door I had my first encounter with Sarah. She was sitting there, right on the back steps crying her eyes out.

"What's wrong with you?" I asked. "Are you hurt?"

"No," she said, "I just want to go home," she sobbed.

"Do you have a mother or a daddy?" I asked her.

"No" she responded.

"Then you don't have a home to go back to, so why don't you just shut up about it."

Sarah looked at me with swollen eyes. "Do you have a mother?" she quizzed.

"No, I don't! She's dead, and I'm glad she's dead, so shut up about it."

Sarah stopped crying. Wiping away the tears from her eyes, she asked "Are you nine?"

"No, I'm not nine! I am eleven. Why do you think I'm nine?" I was really getting disgusted with this girl.

"Well," she said, "I'm nine and I'm bigger than you."

"No, just fatter," I snapped as I walked away.

My mother would have been ashamed of me for being mean to Sarah. What Sarah didn't know was that I had to put up a mean, tough front. Otherwise, I might have to sit right down beside her, and cry right along with her. I would not cry! Not ever!

Starting for the playground, I stopped short to estimate the situation. There were about twenty girls, most of which, looked to be about eight to ten years old. Only one girl looked to be my age. In an instant, I decided that I was in no mood to play with babies, so I traced my steps to the back door, then eased around to the front of the house. Sarah followed.

"You will be in trouble," she warned.

"I've been in trouble my whole life," I answered, and kept walking.

Arriving at the front of the house, I looked towards Winnah's cottage to see if I could spot her. She was nowhere to be seen. Way across campus, a few boys were tossing a ball. Billy and Harley were not among them. I felt so lost and sad, that I decided I just wouldn't think about it, until I was feeling better. By then, I would make some sense of it.

I walked straight into the house, up the steps and down the hall towards that huge bathroom. As I undressed, I saw Sarah out of the corner of my eye. "You will be in trouble," she said again. I ignored her, turned on the water, adjusting it the way the matron, Miss Evelyn, had shown me. Wow! This was heaven! As the warm water sprayed all over me, I couldn't help but think that these orphanage folks, who ever they might be, were rich. There was sweet smelling soap and real shampoo, which I used lavishly. Now I could be shiny clean, just like Wanda Kay.

I put on a clean dress, parted my hair on the side and rolled it with my seven bobby pins. I envisioned my hair looking like that of Miss Coons, except my hair was longer. My envisioning came to a quick halt when Miss Evelyn appeared at the door. The lyrical sound had gone from her voice as she addressed Sarah.

"Where are you supposed to be?"

Sarah slinked away leaving all of Miss Evelyn's attention for me. I didn't know what I had done wrong, but I just knew I was about to get a whipping.

"Come with me," she said.

I followed Miss Evelyn to her room, which was in the corner, directly across the hall from the bathroom.

Miss Evelyn offered me a straight chair as she began to speak.

"Now, Mildred, I know this is your first day and you don't know the rules, so let me explain. From now on, you will not do anything without first asking permission. Here (at the Children's Home), we have a schedule. Meals are eaten at an exact time, three times a day. You will bathe every night, at an exact time. You will do chores at an exact time, get up and go to bed, at an exact time. You will also play at an exact time. If you are playing and need to go to the bathroom, you must first ask permission to come inside. Oh, and one other thing; I expect you to answer "Yes, Ma'am, No Ma'am. Do you understand?"

I understood all right. My Mother had taught me how to talk in a courteous fashion. I surely did not need this old woman to teach me anything.

"Do you understand, Mildred?" she asked again.

"Yes Ma'am," I answered politely.

"Now, there's one other thing, Mildred. It's against the rules for you to roll your hair. As a matter of fact, I have to cut it."

I made a quick decision that I had better be more pliable, or I would find myself looking just like all those girls I saw on the play ground.

"Oh please, don't cut it off. It looks really good when it's dry!" I begged.

"Well, I don't like cutting hair; I don't even know how. I have to put a bowl on the girls heads to get it even," she confessed.

I saw my opportunity and seized it, with a whopping lie.

"I know how to cut hair; I like to cut hair." I assured her. My statement was made so convincingly, that I almost believed it myself.

Besides, a long time ago, I had watched Mother cut hair. I really thought that I could do it.

Miss Evelyn surprised me with her next question.

"Could you cut your own hair?"

"Yes, Ma'am, if you have some good scissors." I lied again.

"What about my hair, do you think you could roll it?" she asked.

I could not believe it! Miss Evelyn actually believed me! So, I lied again.

"Yes Ma'am, I could roll your hair, if I had more bobby pins; I only have seven," I confessed.

"Oh, I use clips, and I have plenty of them. Tomorrow, I might find out if you can do it. Right now, you go out back to the play ground and play with the other girls."

I obeyed by going out back to the playground, but I did not play. I simply watched. Sarah sat next to me and watched too. Thank goodness, she had stopped that stupid crying.

That evening, at bedtime, I almost got into trouble with Miss Evelyn again, when I attempted to go to bed in only my underpants.

"Here, we sleep in our pajamas," she instructed, "not our underwear."

For some reason it scared me to give up my panties. I finally relinquished them, as I decided it was better to lose them than to lose my hair. I didn't dare make Miss Evelyn mad at me.

The next day was Saturday. Some of the girls complained about the cleaning, washing and ironing we had to do. I told them they were sissies. If they had ever picked cotton they would know how easy our chores were. I could see that I wasn't making friends but I didn't care.

Miss Evelyn kept her word and gave me a chance to roll her hair. I was scared to death, but I wouldn't let her know that. After her hair was dry, I prayed hard as I brushed it out. I arranged it as best as I could and handed her the mirror.

"You really can roll hair!" she exclaimed. "You can save me a lot of money at the beauty shop," she said happily.

I thought perhaps I had better seal the deal, while she was still so happy.

"Does this mean I don't have to cut my hair?" I pleaded.

"Well, here are some scissors. See if you can cut it above the shoulders so you won't stand out too much from the other girls."

The compromise of cutting my hair about five inches kept me from getting skinned with a bowl on my head. From then on, Miss Evelyn let me roll her hair and do all the hair cutting of the other girls. Eventually, by trial and error, I learned what I was doing. Eventually, I let the girls' hair grow, just shaping it. Soon, Miss Evelyn bought me lots of bobby pins, allowing me to roll all the girls hair every Saturday.

# THIRTY-SIX

I had not seen Winnah, Billy nor Harley since we arrived on Friday. As we walked to church on Sunday, I heard one of the girls talking about "Campus Hour." At three o'clock every Sunday, all two hundred children got together on that big lawn. From what she said, I gathered that it was a free time, for all the kids to do what they wanted. My heart soared; I heard nothing the preacher said. I just wanted to walk home, have lunch and wait 'til three o'clock.

Campus hour was everything I had imagined. A sea of children filled that big lawn at exactly three o'clock. Some of the children started a baseball game. Most of the children seemed to be playing and visiting with their brothers and sisters. Winnah, Billy, Harley and I found each other and were comparing our new situations, when a big, fat, red haired, snaggle-toothed boy, started chasing me. I didn't like him or any other boys, except my brothers. So I ran. And ran! All I wanted was to be with Winnah and my brothers; this big ugly, boy was keeping me from it. So, I quit running and confronted him.

"What do you want?" I asked in a hateful voice.

"I'm Columbus, and I want you to be my girl friend," he stated.

"Well, I won't," I said firmly.

"Why not?" he asked.

I decided that if I insulted him, he might leave me alone, so I responded, "Cause you're too fat."

Columbus was undaunted. "Okay," he said, "I'll turn all of this fat into muscle; then you will be my girl friend," he insisted as he walked away.

Four o'clock came too soon. At last, by getting rid of Columbus, I had a chance to find out that Winnah was very happy. She liked her matron and everything. Billy and Harley seemed okay too. I just wished I was.

I didn't really like Miss Evelyn, but decided to get along with her, in order to keep my hair. Miss Jesse, our downstairs matron, was a different story. I'm not suggesting she was mean. It was her job to keep us girls on a schedule. It seemed the only time she spoke to us was to direct, or correct us. She organized our house as a sergeant might have demanded precision from his troops. The least goof-up meant being put under restrictions, doing extra chores.

My first restriction came about because I was overheard using profanity. Miss Jesse decided my punishment; it was to shell and net our one gallon of hard shell pecans. An hour later, there was not a single pecan in the jug. Um, were they tasty! As the downstairs hall floor was growing harder by the minute, I decided to comply and fill the jar.

Miss Jesse did have one soft spot. Her name was Cassie, a nine year old, who reportedly had St. Vida's Dance. To my knowledge, Cassie, Miss Jesse's pet, was the only girl who ever went into Miss Jesse's room. She was allowed to play there when the rest of us were working or in bed.

Excursions were rare at the orphanage, mainly due to the shortage of transportation, I'm sure. Shortly before school started, a bus had been borrowed to take us to the Pike County Lake. There must have been forty or fifty of us girls on the bus, along with chaperones and picnic supplies. When we arrived at the lake, I was awed at its beauty and size. It was very large; however, I quickly estimated that I could walk around it in an hour, if I could just sneak away.

While the chaperones were busy unloading the picnic supplies, I quickly slipped into the woods to the right of the lake. Good! There was a trail to follow. I was just thinking about how nice it was to be alone, when I heard a voice behind me.

"You're going to be in trouble!"

Of course, it was Sarah, my unwanted shadow. There she stood, holding her hand to her crotch like she had to pee. She always stood in this weird manner. I demanded that she go back, even threatened to hit her with a stick. Sarah wouldn't budge. If I hit Sarah, I knew she would cry out; the chaperones would discover that we were not with the group. Finally, I walked on, as Sarah continued to follow.

Not having seen a lake before, I had no idea that it wasn't perfectly round. The farther we walked, the more streams we had to wade across. The trail had long since dead-ended. After a long time we found an inlet, or tributary that was too wide and too deep to cross. The only decision was to follow it up stream and find a safe place to cross. By doing this, we went farther and farther from the lake. It occurred to me to go back, but I really thought going back would take longer than continuing ahead. After finding a place to cross, we were in deep woods again! Sarah started that baby crying because she was hungry. I told her I knew the lake was to the left. If we hurried, we would soon be in that beautiful clearing we had seen as we got off the bus.

What I thought would be a short walk turned into several hours. By then it was dusk and Sarah, holding onto a tree, refused to go another step farther.

"I'm scared, I'm scared," she cried.

I was scared too. I knew we were in bad trouble with those orphanage folks, but I knew crying wouldn't help matters.

"I ought to just leave you here," I scolded Sarah. Sarah cried harder.

There was only one choice I could make, so I made it. Leaning forward, I said, "Ride piggy back." Sarah crawled onto my back, arms around my neck. To avoid being choked to death, I supported her weight by placing my arms under her rear end, and locking my hands together. Soon the beautiful day gave way to total darkness. I could not see my feet nor the low branches of the trees that kept cutting me across the face. Utter fear and determination kept me going.

Sarah grew heavier and heavier. I lost one of my shoes as I sank into the marshy bog. I thought to myself, "God, if you are really there, please help me and Sarah. She is just too fat for me to carry much farther."

I stopped dead still where I stood and, dropped Sarah to the ground. I thought I heard someone call my name.

Did God know my name? Making Sarah hush, I listened to make sure that my strong imagination wasn't running wild. There it was again, very faint, but very real.

"Sarah! Mildred!" It surely was a man's voice, but whose?

I hugged Sarah to me. "Now do what you do best, Sarah, cry just as loud and long as you can."

She did. I yelled to the top of my lungs, "Help! Help!"

Help did come. Mr. White and another man who worked for the orphanage said they had been searching for hours. Our rescuers were in a small rowboat that took us to safety. From the middle of the lake, I looked back to the spot where they found us. It was pitch dark and scary. I felt very grateful. Realizing, we had not even made it one fourth of the way around the lake, made me feel foolish. What really puzzled and surprised me was that anyone would bother to look for us.

Minor offenses were handled by the matron. Major offenses were handled by Mr. Cox. The next day, when the girls found out that I was being sent to Mr. Cox, they demonstrated their concern for me. I was surprised that they did not like or trust Old Eagle Eyes. I loved him! The only time I got to see him was in church. Each Sunday morning, he would walk past me, as he helped the other deacons pass the plate, taking the offering.

Mr. Cox looked more stern than usual as I was shown into his office. I could feel his eyes looking at me as I nervously inspected my shoes. Finally, Mr. Cox spoke, "You do realize that you and Sarah could have gotten hurt, or much worse, don't you?"

"Yes, sir," I said, still examining my feet.

"That's an undeveloped area with lots of wild animals. I'm just glad you didn't make it to Cotton Mouth Cove. You and Sarah were less than a mile from there. It's called Cotton Mouth Cove because it's said to be the most snake-infested area in the entire county. You had us all very worried!"

I wanted to say something nice to Mr. Cox, but how could I tell him that I wasn't used to anyone being concerned for me. So, I just stood there.

"Sit down, Mildred and talk to me. You might know by now that most of the children here, don't want to be here. You told me you wanted to come. Have you changed you mind?" he asked.

"No, sir," I honestly responded.

"Then, why do you get into so much trouble?" he asked.

"I don't know," I answered.

"Well, suppose you tell me some of the things you like about being here," he said.

"Well, there's lots to eat. I don't get beatings, and I have real store-bought shampoo and toothpaste - and a toothbrush . . . ," my voice trailed off.

"I see," said Mr. Cox. "Now, tell me what you don't like," he prompted.

I hesitated then blurted, "I want to be with Winnah and Harley and Billy!"

"So, that's it!" Mr. Cox said with an understanding in his voice. "Let me explain. You see, we have to do everything the most efficient, economical way. We don't have enough money nor personnel to let families live together. Do you understand?" he quizzed.

"No, Sir. I thought you were rich."

Mr. Cox laughed, then replied. "All of our money comes from donations from Baptist churches around the state. Without their generosity we would have to close this place."

"Is it welfare?" I asked. "No. It is love and goodness from many, many people," he responded.

Mr. Cox stopped talking and just studied me for a while. Finally he spoke, "I know you don't understand this now, but someday you will. Right now, you just need to settle down and stay out of trouble. You're a smart girl, and pretty too. Do you know . . you remind me of my wife when she was your age! Mrs. Cox was my childhood sweetheart," he explained, then looked at me again for a long time before asking, "Do you have anything to ask me before you go?"

Fearing to ask, I looked at my feet again, then at him. "What is my punishment?"

Mr. Cox laughed. "Most of the children think it is a terrible punishment to have to talk to me, now you just go on back to your cottage," he directed.

Not wanting to go, I slowly slid from the chair and stood to my feet. As I found my way out the door, I thought about my punishment; I deducted that I should commit a major offense more often. I liked talking to Mr. Cox.

# THIRTY- SEVEN

School soon started, with me being an unwilling participant. Most of the time, I had no idea what the teacher was talking about, nor did I care. The year would have been an unmemorable blur, except for the constant trouble I brought on myself. I accepted any and every challenge. When I was dared to jump off a playground swing when it reached its highest point, I did so. The result was a broken arm. As if one cast was not enough, I broke my foot on another senseless dare. Once, three boys double-dog dared me to jump off the high dive into the swimming pool. When I confessed that I could not swim, they withdrew their dare and suggested that I take the ladder back down. I didn't back off.

"No, I won't go back down the ladder and I won't jump. I'll dive," was my sharp response.

"What if you drown?" one of the boys asked.

"I don't care." I said, and recklessly dived into the pool. Once in the water, my survival instincts must have taken over, as I came to the surface dog paddling. Short of breath, but long on pride, I made it to the edge of the pool and climbed out.

There was never a time I wasn't under restrictions . . . for not getting out of bed when the bell rang, for not following rules, for cursing, for picking fights at school.

I developed such a reputation that matrons from other cottages would single me out and declare, "I wish you were in my cottage; I would take you down a notch or two." This was an invitation so I always responded. "Listen here, you old bitch. You can't hurt me! Someday, I'll be big and you'll be old and dead."

Each time I was sent to Mr. Cox. I must have held the record for the kid who was most often punished by being sent to Mr. Cox.

We always walked to school, rain or shine. Sometimes I met up with Billy or Harley and we walked together. Always, always, that pesky Sarah was right behind me. I didn't mind that Harley and Billy had an apple or an orange to take to school, but I resented Sarah for having fruit. Every girl in my cottage took a piece of fruit to school, except me. I didn't understand; I took my discontent out on Sarah. Every morning, I made her give me her fruit, which I promptly ate with no guilt.

My robbery of Sarah was eventually discovered. Again, I was sent to Mr. Cox, who patiently explained that it was the rule of our public school. Every child, ten years old and under, should have fruit for a mid-morning snack, every day. It seemed the orphanage was in trouble because Sarah had been showing up without hers.

"But, I'm the only girl in the cottage that can't have fruit," I complained.

Mr. Cox said, "Mildred, you are the only girl in your cottage who is over ten years old. We will move you to the next cottage as soon as we can. Meanwhile, I want you to understand that we cannot afford fruit for all the children. Here, I want you to read this letter that I just wrote."

I felt so special that he would allow me to read his letter, so I took it. The letter was addressed to a church; it's contents really shocked me as it stated that the orphanage was dangerously low on funds, that it took a great deal of money to feed and house over two hundred children. Mr. Cox was clearly begging for money to be sent quickly.

As I handed the letter back to Mr. Cox, I had to force myself to hold back the tears.

Reading my face, Mr. Cox asked, "What do you think of the letter?"

I never lied to Mr. Cox. I looked him straight in the eye and confessed, "I'm really ashamed of myself; I didn't know you had to beg for money."

"Good," he said, "There's always hope for a child with a conscience. Now, go on back to your cottage."

I left Mr. Cox with a vow in my heart to improve my behavior. I could not tell Mr. Cox that I loved him. Maybe I could show him by not causing him so much trouble.

It was spring. I had just become twelve years old and received my next to last report card for the year. It was terrible, but I didn't care, not until Mr. Cox came to my cottage that evening. He looked at each report card then spoke in a slow, tired voice.

"Your report cards aren't what I expected from you." Then he was silent as though he was thinking. He continued, "I really wish that just one of you girls could make straight A's. Is there anyone who thinks she could?"

Mr. Cox was answered by silence from the group. One at a time he asked several of the girls if they could make all A's with a response of "No, sir," from each. I was just waiting for him to ask me but he didn't. Maybe he thought I wasn't smart enough to make good grades.

As he was rising to leave, I surprised myself by announcing, "I could make straight A's if I wanted to."

With a half smile, Mr. Cox challenged me. "Good, Mildred! I hope you will want to."

To everyone's disbelief, my grades in every subject the last six weeks of the year, were all A's.

That summer I was moved to the next age cottage. In a strange way, I hated leaving Sarah. Somehow, I had grown fond of her and knew I would miss her. Before leaving, I went to the central storage room and took possession of my yellow dress that I had worn to Mother's funeral. Since I had out grown it, Miss Evelyn had passed it down to another girl. As I stuffed it into my sack, Sarah said, "You will be in trouble." I smiled and gave Sarah a big hug.

# THIRTY-EIGHT

The downstairs matron in my new cottage was Mimi Fenn. Winnah had been in her cottage until recently, when she was moved to what we called the baby cottage. An older girl was needed to help take care of the five and six year olds. I wished Winnah wasn't so good at taking care of babies; we might have had a chance to live in the same cottage.

Winnah had told me several times how much she loved Mimi Fenn. I could see why; there was something about her, which reminded me of our Mother. It wasn't her looks, but her manner. She was strict but fair, never showing favoritism. I would rather have taken a whipping than to have her talk to me.

Because I liked Mimi Fenn so much, I really tried to stay out of trouble but trouble found me. Her name was Katie, a fifteen year old, very developed, fat girl with naturally snow-white, curly hair. She called herself Marilyn Monroe. Katie let me know right away she was the head honcho of the cottage, and that I had better do everything she said or else. I had a general idea of what or else meant, but I could not see myself hunkering under to Katie nor her two very large lieutenants.

The very first Sunday after my arrival, Katie decided to test the water, to put me into a position of having to give in to her. It was Sunday lunchtime. The mood was rather formal with two long tables, twelve girls at each table. Our two matrons sat at a small table. My assigned place was at one end of the table. Katie was seated at the opposite end. She obeyed the rules by not talking out loud; she sent an inflammatory message, which was passed to me one girl at a time. I did not blame the girls who passed the message, just Katie who sent it. So, I sent back a message of my own which was passed to her one girl at a time. The message was, "You're about to find this water pitcher between your teeth."

Katie received the message and passed back to me, "You don't have the guts to do it," believing that I would not risk getting into trouble.

I passed no more messages. I picked up the water pitcher and slammed it, ice and all, down the long table, right into Katie's face.

Of course, I missed lunch that day, and campus hour, and everything else for weeks to come. I also received a lecture from Mimi Fenn about self-control. I didn't understand why I was in trouble, under restrictions, but Katie wasn't. Just the same, I decided I would never give in to Katie, no matter how many extra chores I had to do. Restriction chores were done in addition to regular work.

All boys, over twelve years of age, worked the fields, growing anything we could eat. Gracious, we ate a lot of black-eyed peas! The boys also milked the cows and delivered a five-gallon can of milk to the back door of each cottage, every morning. The boys of the orphanage also kept that large campus mowed; that's why it always looked so nice.

Girls, twelve and older, had their duties too. We kept the administration building clean. We also cut and bundled coupons and worked in the laundry. For awhile, I and several other girls, scissors cut, counted and bundled coupons. These coupons were sent from all over the state of Alabama. Some people actually trimmed them; others just tore them out and stuck them in the mail. It didn't matter; they were worth money. Some coupons were worth one mill; others were worth three or five mills. Occasionally, we found one worth a penny, or five whole cents. The Children's Home turned in these coupons for cash. Eventually, we had enough to build a small infirmary, where those of us who were sick, could go to recover. To keep contagious things like mumps, flu and measles from spreading, visitors were not usually allowed.

After a time, I was rotated to laundry duty. Underwear and dresses were done by each individual girl's cottage but the central laundry washed and ironed all the sheets. The boys did no laundry. Shirts, pants, sheets, everything was done by central laundry. Teams of two girls each folded the sheets to perfection. I enjoyed this in a way. My problem came about, when I was assigned to the large steamers. Each time, I folded the pant legs just as I was instructed, for the perfect crease. Then I was supposed to reach for the handle, pull it down, and hold it for a few seconds. The problem was, that I could not reach the handle. I had to jump to grab it. Many times I burned my arm. I would not cry, so I cursed instead. Miss McCullough, the head of the laundry, did not like my cursing.

One day, after several warnings, she said, "Listen here, you jack-ass."

I defended myself, "If I'm a jackass, you are a double jackass."

Miss McCullough's reaction was one of surprise and anger. I truly thought she would hit me. Instead, she sternly ordered, "Come outside!" I followed her out the door.

Miss McCullough stood silent for a while. I think she was so mad at me that she was trying to pull herself together. Finally, she said, "I am going to say this to you just once. I think that you have potential but you are doing yourself in, with your ugly mouth. You need to learn to shut up and get along! And another thing, if someone who is in charge of you says something that you know is untrue, you can think anything you wish, just don't say it. Shut your mouth and just say, Yes, ma'am." She hesitated. "Let me show you what I mean!" "Do you see that beautiful, black stallion standing there in the pasture?" she asked. I looked across the road, past the barbed fence to see an old gray mare standing there. Miss McCullough and I looked at each other. I believed she must be playing a game with me.

Eventually, I caught on, "Yes, ma'am, I see that beautiful black stallion standing in the pasture." Miss McCullough never spoke directly to me again. I never again cursed when I burned my arms with the steamers. Somehow, we were friends. We had reached an understanding.

# THIRTY-NINE

The end of summer was nearing when Lash La Rue came to town. He was my favorite cowboy! He used a whip instead of a gun. Now, when a young girl has a crush on a movie star, there is no way she can miss her only chance to see him. It is a matter of the heart that no adult can understand. That was my problem. Mimi Fenn didn't understand that I would simply die if I didn't see him. No amount of pleading nor begging netted me, what was considered to be, an extra privilege.

Undaunted, I begged our Sunday school teacher to have a party for us, taking us to see Lash La Rue. She refused. Couldn't anyone see how important this was? Couldn't they see that my heart would break into little pieces? As a last resort, I got permission to go to Mr. Cox. He would understand! He understood all right! He understood that I was trying to circumvent Mimi Fenn's authority. It hurt my feelings that Mr. Cox caught on to me so easily.

My determination was stronger than ever. I tried to follow the rules! If no one would understand, then I would just have to break the rules, go without permission. In discussing it with my new friend, Mary, we concocted a simple, secret plan. Slip out!

That Friday night, after everyone was in bed, Mary and I met in the storage room. Although it was too warm to wear them, we slipped lightweight coats over our pajamas and was out the window in a flash. We slid down a column to the ground floor, as though we had done it hundreds of times before. Now, the next step was to actually get to the movie theater, which was a mile away. There were only two possible routes. Elm Street was the main road, but it was not a consideration. Some nosy townsperson would be sure to see us, and promptly call Mr. Cox.

The alternate road was very dangerous but perfect for two girls who did not want to be seen. As we walked the narrow dirt road lined with run down shacks we had several scares from dogs. We encountered an obnoxious drunk who tried to grab us. Escaping his clutches, we broke into a run, only to have another drunk yell at us from his front stoop. Lucky for us, he fell down his steps and landed face down. We dared not help him, lest we ended up needing help ourselves. We knew this was a part of town where even the police didn't go, except in the daytime.

We did make it to the theater. Since Mary was much taller than I, she bought the tickets. Keeping her chin down, Mary never showed her eyes and face, which was partly hidden by a boy's cap. We entered the theater and took seats on the very back row. Good! We had not been seen! The second show was already underway, and all eyes were fixed on Lash La Rue.

There he was, dressed all in black, including his gaucho hat, adorned with a band of sparkling silver medallions. His large, silver belt buckle glistened, projecting rays of light into the dark theater. I was so excited that I felt I might faint. Of course, the hot coat may have had something to do with it. Was I hot! I removed the coat displaying my pajamas. After all, no one could see us in the dark movie house.

Lash La Rue was all that I expected. He performed unbelievable feats. The cracking of his whip, like the sound of gun fire, echoed from all corners of the room. The trick I liked best, was when he cut a cigarette in half. His assistant, who held the cigarette in his mouth, showed no fear.

The show, a promotional performance hyping his movie, was over all too soon. We stayed in our seats as planned, waiting for the audience to clear out. Many people did leave, but many others stayed, trying to get backstage. Oh, how I wanted to join them, to be face to face with my idol. The certainty of being recognized and told on was a fact, not just an uncertain possibility. My hero would have to go through the rest of his life, never knowing how much he was adored.

The road home was just as dangerous and scary, but somehow it didn't matter very much. We had accomplished our goal perfectly. No one would ever know our secret. It was as though Mary and I were invisible, totally undetected.

The next day, every girl in the house knew every detail of our adventure. Mary had told! Moreover, under Mary's leadership, they had made plans to go to see Lash La Rue's final performance. I begged Mary not to go.

"Twenty-three girls are too many; you're bound to be noticed," I reasoned.

"Twenty-three? You would make twenty-four. Aren't you going?" she asked.

"No, I think it's dumb, because you will be caught."

They were caught! The whole house, except for me, was in trouble. At bed check, I was the only one found to be in bed. Nevertheless, our matrons eyed me suspiciously since I was the one who had begged so long to see Lash La Rue. Every time they looked at me, I put on my best angelic face.

I hated it that Mary was in trouble, but I relished in the fact that Katie and her lieutenants were right there with her. I'm sure Katie wanted to tell on me, but she would have broken the code, losing her status forever. The code was simple, "Never tell on each other."

# FORTY

The most awaited, expectant time of the whole year was vacation time. It was the time around which the entire orphan's year evolved! For two whole weeks, the forty-acre campus of the orphanage was silent of children's laughter, tears or chores. A lucky few went to visit relatives. The large majority took potluck, being sent all around the state to whomsoever requested a boy or girl of a particular age. It was an adventure that the boys and girls talked about all year long.

I watched as Billy's name was pinned to his left shoulder. He had been promised to a family in Mobile, Alabama, a long bus trip for a little boy all alone. I wanted to go with him, to protect him. Of course that couldn't happen. The family who requested him asked for a sweet, seven-year-old boy. Their request did not include a twelve year old, hateful girl. Winnah and Harley were on totally different buses. I knew practically nothing about public buses and certainly had no reason to be concerned. It's just that I was afraid Billy and Harley could get lost.

A family in Vinemont, Alabama had apparently requested two pre-teen girls. My friend, Irene, and I seemed to fit that request, so I had a travel mate. What great happenings were in store for us? I envisioned us going to movies, shopping, swimming, or maybe we would have a wiener roast. I could hardly contain myself.

Our wildest imaginations could not have prepared us for the next two weeks. Every morning and every evening we spent in a small rural church, attending revival meetings. In between church services, we spent our time trying to avoid our requested family's two weird sons. The younger one liked to hide under our bed, or in the closet, to watch us change clothes. The older one was about seventeen, past the age of looking. Roland's approach was more hands-on.

The only way we could avoid Roland's advances was to stay close to his mother's side. She was an industrious woman who filled her time by cleaning house, preparing meals or weeding the garden. We protected ourselves by helping her. "You girls sure do like to work," Mrs. Smith often remarked.

One afternoon Mrs. Smith asked Irene to fetch fresh turnips from the garden. Irene complied, making her way out the back door and taking a short cut through the corn field. I made up an excuse to go outside, as I was concerned for Irene. My concern became a quick reality as I saw Roland chasing Irene, catching up to her, and wrestling her down to the ground right between the cornrows.

I don't remember thinking about what to do, or where I got the big stick that I found in my hand. I just remember fraling the daylights out of Roland until he got off of Irene and limped away. Wow! I reminded myself of Aunt Lorez!

Irene and I had had enough of this vacation. We would have gone back to the orphanage immediately but that was against the rules. We had no choice but to stick it out. One thing was for certain; we would never admit to our friends at the home what a miserable time we had. Instead, we would make up stories about our grand, wonderful experiences. Of course, our lying made me wonder, how many of the other kids were lying too.

Over two hundred children returned from vacation, safe and sound. All except one. After checking on Billy, Harley and Winnah, my next concern was for Sarah, who was nowhere to be found. With permission, I went to my former matrons, Miss Jessie and Miss Evelyn. Miss Jessie, as usual, would tell me nothing. Miss Evelyn said only that she had gone to a far worse place.

Without permission, I went to see my Mr. Cox, assured that he would explain Sarah's far worse place. Mr. Cox answered my question by asking me a question.

"If you had to go back to your grandparents would you consider that to be a far worse place?"

Shivering at the thought, I quickly answered, "Yes, sir, but why did Sarah have to go back?"

Mr. Cox always answered questions in a measured fashion, "Because, Mildred, Sarah could not adjust. Any child who cannot fit in here, has to leave. Sometimes they go back to relatives; sometimes they go into foster care."

I really wanted to ask Mr. Cox what foster care meant, but I decided to end the conversation before he discovered that I was there without permission. I certainly did not want to be shipped off to a far worse place.

Columbus, my would-be boy friend, had not bothered me since that first campus hour. He seemed to watch me at a distance, occasionally sending me Clove chewing gum. He always sent it by one of his friends. Before sending it, he always tore off the letter C so the wrapper read love. I wondered how Columbus could afford to lavish fine gifts of love chewing gum on me, when he only made fifteen cents per week. All the younger children received the same amount each week, but were required to give two cents of it to church. That was our ten percent tithe.

One Sunday afternoon during campus hour, a heavy package was handed to me by another of Columbus's friends. I opened the package to find a brand new pair of roller skates, key included. Without thinking, I headed for the nearest sidewalk, sat down on the ground adjusting and strapping them to my feet. It never occurred to me that I might fall, so I didn't. It was as though I was floating on air, as I swayed, turned, and rolled up and down the sidewalk, just like my old friend Wanda Kay.

I wondered how Columbus had gotten the money to buy the skates, or if he had indeed bought them. I didn't want to think about that, I would just thank him. I was just trying to figure out how to thank Columbus for the finest gift of my whole life, when Mary approached me.

Mary appeared anxious and agitated as she exclaimed, "Katie said for you to come up there, right now!"

Katie and her two strong arms being under restrictions, were grounded to their room. Somehow, Katie blamed me for their plight. I didn't bother to ask Mary why they wanted to see me. I knew all too well.

Suddenly, my legs felt like wet noodles. I found myself lying on the sidewalk, as Mary asked, "What are you going to do?" I could not give voice to that question, but, in my heart, I knew there were only two choices. I could face them and be beaten to an inch of my life or I could just not go at all. I knew that if I did not face them, I would have to hunker under to Katie from then on.

"Better to be dead than to be owned," I told Mary as I removed my skates.

"Don't go! Don't go! They will kill you!" she warned.

As I walked across that big lawn, toward my cottage, I tried to think of a way to defend myself. The only thing that came into my head was that Katie and her two friends weighed about one hundred and thirty pounds each. I weighed about eighty nine pounds soaking wet. In my mind's eye, I could picture the three of them laying in wait for me, ready to pounce on me. I felt like a soldier going into battle with no weapon, outnumbered and powerless to defend a principle that I held so dear.

Too numb with fear to devise a plan, my old survival instincts must have kicked in as I approached the closed door to the bedroom. Instead of gently opening the door, I yanked it open and jumped on the first of the twelve beds. Without knowing it, I had apparently wound the leather straps of the skates tightly around my hands. Instinctively, I waved the skates in circular motions around my head. I became a jumping jack as I sprang from bed to bed hitting them anywhere I could with my shiny new skates. Of course, the three girls eventually overpowered me, paying me back for each and every one of their bruises and cuts.

The four of us were bloody messes when our upstairs matron heard the ruckus and broke up the fight. I was in a small amount of trouble for having gone up to the room without permission. Katie and the other two girls were in a huge amount of trouble for demanding that I come.

In the days that followed, I gradually came to the realization that Katie actually felt threatened by me. Her demeanor gave me cause to believe that she was waiting on me to take over her position as head girl of the cottage. After all, I had won the fight! How she came to that conclusion was beyond me! All I wanted was to be left alone. I had no desire to control the other girls, to take their candy, or make them do my chores. Besides, I was too little to be a queen bee.

I got my wish. Life became much easier as Katie and I coexisted without speaking. She and her friends left me alone; I was all too glad to return the same favor.

# FORTY-ONE

School soon started and I found myself going to a different school, the same as Winnah. We only had two schools, elementary and high school. Elementary was grades one through six. High school was grades seven through twelve. Being a big seventh grader, I was now in high school. Determined to make Mr. Cox proud of me, I vowed to myself to stay out of trouble and continue making straight A's. Further, I decided to quit getting placed under restrictions, by getting out of bed on time.

Each and every morning, from down stairs, Mimi Fenn rang a small bell three times and each morning she yelled, "Rise and shine!" Exactly five minutes later, each girl was expected to be dressed, have her bed made, teeth brushed and on her job. The problem was that I never heard the bell! When the five minute check was made, I was still in bed. I devised a plan to stay awake all night so that I could hear the bell. My plan worked! I actually got up and was on my job in five minutes. The negative side of my plan was witnessed by all of my classmates and teachers when I slept all day in class. After a few days, I began to realize that I was defeating myself. How could I make straight A's if I couldn't keep my eyes open?

For the first time in my life, I realized that I needed help. It was mighty hard but I swallowed my independent pride, asking two of my friends to get me out of bed every morning. I was asking a great deal and I knew it. By helping me, they could miss their five minute deadline, ending up in trouble themselves.

Each morning Mary dragged me out of bed while Frances ran to the bathroom for a wet rag. A slap in the face with a cold, wet bath cloth half woke me enough to sleep walk through the morning procedure. I was very grateful to Mary and Frances but more grateful that they did not get caught helping me.

Most of the girls in my cottage were afraid to associate with me, much less, befriend me. Although she permanently ignored me, Katie still bullied most of the other girls. I believe that she threatened them not to have anything to do with me. This was a problem. On one hand, they were afraid not to obey Katie. On the other hand, they wanted me to do their hair. So, I had to think of a plan that would allow me to fix their hair, and keep them out of trouble with Katie, at the same time.

I had noticed coupons on our Nifty notebook paper that we were given for our school work. Under the coupon read: Save these coupons and win a shiny new bicycle. The fine print was not quite that encouraging. It seemed to indicate that the one boy and one girl from the whole United States who sent in the most coupons were the winners. It sounded like a long shot but what if I won? I could already feel the wind in my face and the freedom of speed as I thought about the beauty of a sleek, red bike.

My twelve year old daydreaming snapped back to reality as I suddenly knew this was the perfect plan to foil Katie. The girls would have to give me Nifty coupons as payment, in exchange for my doing their hair. They could pretend no friendship. The best part of my plan was that the coupons had no value to anyone except me. In the past, they had all been thrown away.

I had continued to do my former matron, Miss Evelyn's, hair - plus I cut the hair of all her charges. Now, in my new cottage, everyone wanted me to do their hair. Soon, the girls and matrons from two other cottages wanted my haircuts.

I wondered if it was the coupons or my ability that brought about my thriving business. The bottom line was, that I could not accommodate over one hundred girls plus twenty or more matrons every Saturday. Monday through Friday I went to school, then worked in the laundry in the afternoons. There just wasn't enough time!

Maybe the girls complained! Maybe the matrons went to Mr. Cox. I have no idea how it came about, but I was removed from the laundry and reassigned to my own beauty shop.

Words cannot describe my exultation! My shop was just a little corner of the sewing room. The sewing room was a small building behind Miss Jessie's cottage. Mrs. Robinson, a very sweet woman, was the only seamstress on campus. She kept our clothes repaired as best as she could with only one sewing machine.

When I arrived on my new job, Mrs. Robinson welcomed me with real enthusiasm. She told me that she had been lonely working with no one else around.

To make sure I felt welcome, Mrs. Robinson had already cleaned out my corner, furnishing it with one wooden straight chair. I felt like Cinderella in her fine castle. Cutting hair was fun. No longer would I burn my arms in the laundry. Best of all, I now had my own place. I felt like a very fortunate girl!

My fortunate feeling soon turned to one of guilt. I was being rewarded when I knew I did not deserve it.

Just a week before, I had picked a fight with two, big tenth grade boys. They became so mad that they started chasing me across the gym floor. I ran for the nearest exit, locking the door behind me. The boys put all their raging brawn into the door. "Uh-oh! I had better get out of the building!" Looking around, I found that I was on a small, cement landing that took a sharp turn to the left, with nothing but steps and a metal guard rail leading downward. The sound of splashing water and boy's laughing voices floated upwards. I was trapped. There was no way I could escape to the boy's locker room!

Knowing the door could give way at any moment, I pressed my hands tightly to the door knob and walked my legs up the iron railing. Good! My small size was perfect for forming a wedge. Now there was no way my angry pursuers could break the lock. From my horizontal perch, I felt a little safer as I envisioned my body as being a steel rod. Surely the boys would soon grow tired and just give up. To my dismay, they did not abandon the contest. They continued to push and beat on the door until it ripped right off at the hinges!

Lucky for me, one of our coaches arrived on the scene, just as the door split away. He unceremoniously marched the three of us to the principals office, detailing to Dr. Smart all that he had witnessed. Of course, the coach had only seen one side of the door.

The more the boys blamed the damaged door on me, the harder Dr. Smart laughed. "You mean to tell me that a small girl like that could knock down a door all by herself?" I put on my best, sweet face!

Knowing that I had won the contest felt pretty good until I heard the boys groan with pain from the hard paddling they got from Dr. Smart. Why had I done such a thing? My Mother's face passed over my mind, as though she was terribly ashamed of me. At that moment, I really wanted to volunteer that I was responsible for the whole thing, that the boys were telling the truth. Of course, I couldn't, lest I get shipped off from the orphanage.

# FORTY- TWO

One afternoon, Mr. Cox sent word for me to come to his office. "Oh, no! Was Mr. Cox on to me?" He had a way of knowing things and a way of asking straight out questions like, "Now, Mildred, I want to know if you had any part in ripping down the school door?" Dr. Smart did not ask me, or I might have confessed. There was no might about it, where Mr. Cox was concerned. I could never, ever lie to him.

My heart was heavy as I entered Mr. Cox's office. I just knew I was about to be shipped off to that far worse place.

To my surprise, Mr. Cox beamed the biggest smile I had ever seen on his face. He came around his desk, took me by the hand, and led me to the chair.

"Congratulations," he said. "I've just heard that you are the only child on the whole campus to bring home a straight A report card! I'm proud that you're really trying!"

"Yes sir," I said to him. To myself I thought, "If you only knew."

Mr. Cox leaned back in his big chair, looking very pleased with me. "Mildred, when children really try, good things usually happen to them. Do you understand?"

"No sir," I replied.

Leaning forward, Mr. Cox picked up a piece of paper. "I have no idea how they heard about you, but a group of people want to come here to help you with your beauty shop."

Mr. Cox seemed excited. My heart sank. I felt like this group, who-ever they were, would intrude or take away my new found, private corner.

"I don't need any help," I said coldly.

"Well, I can see that you don't understand," Mr. Cox said as he reviewed the letter. "It says right here that they want to bring equipment like a shampoo bowl, a hair dryer, and a real barber's chair. They are donating these things just because of you."

I had never seen any of those things that Mr. Cox was naming, but I had a general idea what they meant. I deducted that this group, with all their fancy equipment, would take over my job, putting me back into the laundry.

Mr. Cox continued, "They say that they can come for only one day, asking if a week from Monday would be all right. They are also requesting that you be excused from school that day. What do you think of this idea?"

With a sigh of relief, I responded in my best grown up voice, "I think one day will be fine. Who are these people?"

Mr. Cox referred to the letter again, "They are members of the Cosmetology Association of the State of Alabama."

With wings on my feet and joy in my heart, I skipped all the way back to my shop. These folks not only sounded well intentioned, they also sounded mighty important. I wondered what cosmetology meant! I would look it up! Meanwhile, I knew they couldn't take my job if they were coming for only one day.

During the next week and a half, I read everything I could get my hands on about cosmetology. I surely did not want to appear ignorant to these important people.

Mrs. Robinson and I threw out, cleaned out, making room for the upcoming expansion. Mr. White installed a hot and cold water line in preparation for the shampoo bowl. I felt so important, when he asked me where I wanted it. This was the same Mr. White who had rescued me and Sarah when we were lost at the lake.

The big day finally came. At eight o'clock sharp, a shiny blue Chevrolet and a small truck pulled up in front of the administration building. Mr. Cox had asked me to be on hand to help welcome the group, but all I could get out of my mouth was a simple, "Hello." I surprised myself at how small and insignificant I felt in the presence of these five, beautiful ladies. It was further humbling to realize they were there because of me.

Mr. Cox suggested that I ride with the ladies, directing them to the sewing room. I was delighted!

Mr. White and another man were already there, waiting to unload the equipment. They had it set up in minutes!

Mrs. Robinson, the five ladies and I unloaded boxes and boxes of supplies that were labeled permanent wave, shampoo, conditioner and rollers. They had even brought hair clips and special hair cutting scissors that were presented to me. My usual big mouth suddenly changed to a small, squeaky, mouse-like sound that mumbled, "Thank you." I was overwhelmed!

Mrs. Robinson served coffee while the ladies set up workstations, doing their best to figure out how to work in so small a space. Not knowing how to help them, I held on to the barber chair, pumping it with my foot, watching it go up and down.

As planned, our school excused ten girls every hour. They had to walk home, shampoo their hair and get to the sewing room with their own towel. The plan worked perfectly, allowing the hairdressers to do more heads. Gracious! I had never seen hands move so fast! They laughed and joked with the girls. Snip! Snip and they were done. I volunteered to keep the hair swept up, as I watched every move they made. As the day went on, I gradually regained my voice and began asking questions, particularly about those pungent, permanent waves. They taught me a great deal. With their supervision, I also gave someone a permanent.

Right in the middle of this momentous procedure, a photographer from the local newspaper showed up! This special day was given prominence as our picture showed up the following day on the front page.

About mid afternoon, my newfound friends learned something from me. Lois, a beautiful ten year old, had naturally curly, dark hair. The hairdresser, who was about to trim her hair, immediately noticed that it had, in the past, been cut shorter on the right side than on the left.

I was elated! Grabbing Lois, I hugged her saying excitedly "See there! See there! I told you no one would notice your crooked neck, if I cut your hair uneven!"

All the hairdressers stopped work long enough to examine Lois's neck, that leaned dramatically to the right, and how I had solved the problem. They seemed impressed. The hairdresser kept the uneven hair cut, but showed me how to layer it to encourage Lois's natural curl.

At the end of the day, the beautiful ladies had given at least thirty permanent waves, cut and set countless heads of hair. They apologized that they could not get to everyone but assured me that they were leaving all the unused supplies, even the permanent waves.

As the ladies were packing up to leave they continued to instruct me. "Don't let anyone use your scissors. They're for cutting hair only. Did we tell you that cutting paper and such will ruin them?"

I believe that the ladies hated to leave as much as I hated to see them go.

That night, my eyes were wide open, as I listened to my eleven roommates make the usual sleeping sounds. I thought about the entire day from beginning to end. Then I tried to figure out why I felt so good when I was so physically tired. An old feeling of self reliance seemed to have popped right into my heart. I had not known this feeling since before our mother became ill.

Tuesday morning I returned to school with my heart brimming over with happy songs. I felt as special as Mother said I was a long time ago. I felt certain that I would never pick another fight. I would stay out of trouble and make all A's for my Mr. Cox.

Alas, my good behavior lasted less than a month.

# FORTY-THREE

Miss Garner, my English teacher, had never been friendly to me, nor any of the kids from the Home. That was okay; we were used to that.

Miss Garner really knew her subject! Spelling, sentence structure, conjugation, were passions of hers. Some of my classmates thought she was too passionate about this English thing. I didn't! Diagramming sentences was fun for me.

One afternoon, Miss Garner announced that she was giving a different kind of test. Seven students at a time would go to the black board. She, then, would give each student a different question. Each student would write his or her answer on the board and be graded on the spot. "There will be absolutely no talking," Miss Garner warned.

The names of six students had already been called. They went to the blackboard and picked up their chalk. Mine was the seventh name Miss Garner called. I walked to the board with confidence, as I knew I had studied. I was ready!

When I arrived at the blackboard, I noticed that there was no more chalk, only six pieces in all. The girl next to me saw my predicament and started to break hers to share with me. Miss Garner stopped her. I truly believed that Miss Garner did not understand the situation so I said, "I have no chalk."

Miss Garner yelled at me, "I said there would be no talking! Mildred, you will get the first question."

I listened to the question; I knew the answer, but could not write it without chalk.

I still believed that Miss Garner would do the fair thing, so I spoke up again. "Miss Garner, may I borrow some chalk?"

On Miss Garner's face was the meanest expression I had ever seen as she responded in a voice that was even meaner. Walking toward me she declared, "Mildred, you get a zero, a goose egg."

As Miss Garner drew a great big zero on the board, something terrible came over me. Something in me must have snapped. Like a volcanic eruption, a steady stream of obscenities was pouring from my mouth. I could not stop the rushing hot lava of profanity even though I was gradually awakening to the situation.

Meanwhile, the color completely drained from Miss Garner's face, leaving her deathlike. When her color returned, her face became bright maroon. I was still so furious that I could hardly make out what she was saying; the gist was, that the class should go to the playground.

I don't remember how long my tirade lasted, but when I came to my full senses, I found myself standing next to my goose egg, completely alone. For some reason, I just stood there. After a while our principal, Dr. Smart, came into the room, followed by Miss Garner. Dr. Smart approached me, demanding that I apologize to Miss Garner. I stood mute. No matter what he said, no matter what he demanded, I refused to respond. Dr. Smart finally retreated from the room.

As soon as he left, Miss Garner grabbed me by the arm, practically dragging me to my desk. Pushing me into the desk, she said, "Now you can just sit there until you are ready to apologize. Don't tell me that you are thirsty, or need to go to the bathroom. Don't move, cough or sleep. Raise your hand only for permission to apologize." My abuser was now my captor!

I sat almost motionless for an hour or two. Then, I heard the bell ringing. All the students would be going home, except me. Good! Now, Mr. Cox would find out what happened. He would come to my rescue, setting my tormentor straight. Choosing his words carefully, he would explain to Miss Garner that I was a very special girl, that I should be treated with respect.

My imagination went wild as I considered all the things my Mr. Cox might say or do to Miss Garner. Miss Garner munched on her snacks, just glaring at me. I smiled back at her as I pictured Mr. Cox arriving with police officers. In my mind's eye, the policemen promptly handcuffed her, hauling her off to jail.

The bright, sun-shiny day slowly gave way to dusk, then total darkness. I had long since finished all of my homework. Now I occupied my time by drawing pictures of horses. Sketching was not among my talents. I just liked horses. I thought about my favorite horse story, Black Beauty, as I tried to ignore the growling of my stomach and my urgent need to go to the bathroom. I knew Miss Garner would not allow me to relieve myself until I first apologized, so I didn't ask to be excused. I was not about to allow myself to have an accident either, for this would have given her additional power over me. Mentally, I watched myself climb on the back of Black Beauty. Without so much as the sound of hoofs hitting the ground, he carried us both to freedom.

It was almost nine o'clock in the evening when Mr. Cox finally arrived. Without ceremony, without police officers, without emotion he simply said, "Go to the car, Mildred. I'll be out shortly."

I obeyed. I ran out of the schoolhouse as fast as my legs would carry me, stopping at the nearest bush in an attempt to end my agony. To my amazement, I could not pee at all! Visions of Daddy sprang to my mind as I recalled the forced singing, the holding of my water for so long that I was in terrible pain.

As Mr. Cox had not yet appeared at the door, I squatted again, managing to squeeze out two small drops. I pulled up my panties as I studied a very bright moon overhead. Without thinking, I stood my tallest and placed my right hand over my heart. "I see the moon and the moon sees me, so now I will make a pledge to thee. I swear to you that someday I will be big and nobody, not anyone, will ever hurt me or my brothers and sisters again."

I was grateful that Mr. Cox stayed in the building for a while. He was talking to Miss Garner, defending me, I supposed. It gave me time to walk around until my kidneys unlocked, ending my pain.

Mr. Cox was very quiet as he drove towards home. Halfway there, he did ask, "Are you aware that you've been expelled?"

"No, sir. I don't think I should be." I answered very matter-of-factly. Mr. Cox did not respond. He drove straight to my cottage and led me to Mimi Fenn's sitting room. "Good! " I thought. Now he would see my side and surely take retribution against Miss Garner.

The three of us sat down as Mr. Cox said "Now, Mildred, suppose you tell me the whole story." So I did! I told Mr. Cox the exact truth about how Miss Garner had mistreated me, and my violent reaction to her unfairness. The only thing I left out, were the actual ugly profane words I had used. I honestly admitted that I could not remember all the bad words, but even if I could, I would not want to repeat them to him.

Mr. Cox looked at me for a long time. While I was waiting for him to speak, I noticed how quiet and dark our cottage was. All my cottage mates were asleep. An eerie feeling came over me, as the lateness of the hour seemed to punctuate my problem.

Mr. Cox finally spoke in his usual, thoughtful manner, "Mildred, I am of the opinion that anyone who is worth a grain of salt, possesses a temper. You have a temper. The only problem is, that you use it in a very destructive manner. Maybe you're too young to realize it, but this tendency can ruin your whole life, as well as the lives of Winnah, Harley and Billy. You know that you have to fit in here, in order to stay. What you may not know, is that if you have to go, your brothers and sister also have to go. What do you think of that?"

Defensively, I blurted, "I think you are taking her side because you don't really understand how mean she was to me."

"Mildred, I believe that Miss Garner was certainly unfair to you, but you should have come to me instead of trying to handle it yourself. Can't you see that the Children's Home is in a precarious situation? On one hand, we have the town kids; on the other hand, we have the home kids. We have to peacefully co-exist in order to be welcome in the local church and public schools. It's a public relations matter; we have to get along with all the townspeople, the good ones and the not so good ones."

"Now, about your expulsion . . . Miss Garner has agreed to let you back in school if you will, the minute the first bell rings, apologize to her and the entire class."

At that moment I thought I would die. If I had any tears, which I hadn't for years, I would have shed them all over myself to drown my disappointment in Mr. Cox. He was asking me to discard my principles for the good of the orphanage. I looked at Mr. Cox straight in the eye and said "I can't do that, I can't apologize."

"Can't or won't?" Mr. Cox questioned.

"Both," I said firmly.

Just as firmly Mr. Cox informed me, "Well then, I suppose I will just have to make other arrangements for you, your brothers and Winnah. You can't stay here."

My Mr. Cox had deserted me! Because of me, the four of us were about to get shipped off to that far worse place, wherever that was. Oh God, what was I to do!

Instinctively, I started talking. A frenzy of words poured from my mouth, the likes of which was probably never heard before or since. As best as I could make sense of my own oratory, it had something to do with how I knew I had improved, and that I knew I could improve a great deal more, if given the chance.

Like a cornered animal, I came out fighting. I continued my verbal defense until somehow, I convinced Mr. Cox that I should be allowed to apologize to the class, but not to Miss Garner.

How he pulled it off, I will never know. All I know is that Mr. Cox drove me to school the next morning. Not a word was spoken until we reached the door of Dr. Smart's office. "Stay here," Mr. Cox instructed me, as he reached for the doorknob.

It seemed like a long time passed before the door reopened. Miss Garner exited, brushing right past me. The door re-opened with a tired looking Mr. Cox leaving this time. "You have only three minutes before the first bell. Get on to class and do what you promised."

Not only did I apologize to the class, but also I tried to do it in such a way that Mr. Cox would be proud. I mimicked him as I measured my words in a clear, distinct voice, being careful not to mention Miss Garner or say anything to offend her further.

When report card time came, I had excellent grades in every class, except Miss Garner's. Miss Garner had the final revenge.

# FORTY-FOUR

Winnah, Billy, Harley and I were safe for now. I knew that just one more major offense from me would cause us all to get shipped off. I tried really hard not to start a fight, nor to react to disagreeable situations. I tried to be very passive, but that just wasn't my nature. So, when I found myself about to react to an unfair situation, I just bit my lip to remind me of the consequences of saying what I thought.

One Sunday, our preacher said, "If you ask Jesus to come into your heart, he will save you, even change you." Now, I knew that no child on earth needed changing more than I. It just seemed impossible. I really wanted to walk down that long aisle and tell the preacher how badly I needed to change, to ask Jesus to come into my heart, to turn me into a better person. My legs wouldn't move!

I just kept my mouth shut and walked back to campus. Quietly, I made it through lunch and the clean up of the dishes.

There was a little free time before campus hour started, which I usually spent skating. This day I could not think of skating, nor campus hour.

When I felt that it was safe to do so, I sneaked off campus and disappeared into the woods. I located my favorite tree, which I had climbed several times before. It was a stately black oak, the tallest in the whole forest. I mounted it and struggled to the top.

"God! Are you there God?" I listened for an answer but all I heard was the wind rustling through the trees. "Mother said you were there, God," I yelled to the top of my lungs. Then, more quietly, I sobbed, "I really need your help, God. I'm a hateful, mean girl. Because of me, we might all get shipped off. I need Jesus to come into my heart and take away the hate. Please God. I can't do it by myself."

I found myself crying, the first time since my daddy sexually abused me. Unrestrained, I cried for my beautiful mother, for her painful suffering and her untimely death. I cried for my siblings, for the abuse they had endured. Lastly, I cried for myself.

Unknown to me at the time, that was the last tree that I would ever climb. As I made my way back to campus, I felt a peace that I had never before known. For the first time in my life I felt that everything would really work out okay for my brothers, my sister and me.

The next Sunday I joined the church. There was no more crying, but there was a great big smile on my face and joy in my steps, as I walked down the aisle, extending my hand to our preacher.

Already interested in my beauty shop, I became more interested in my customers. By making the girls look pretty, they actually felt better about themselves. Some of the girls confided in me their problems as I did their hair. I surprised myself by listening, even making suggestions. It was not surprising to learn that most of the girls had been in very deprived, abusive situations before coming to the orphanage. Their matter of fact stories involved rape, incest, beatings and hunger. It troubled me to know that there were so many mean adults in the world that preyed on children. Sometimes, when they asked me, "Why?" I found myself repeating my Mother's words. "That's just the way it is. Don't let it ruin your life."

The desire to fight, to easily take offense had mysteriously left me. What really shocked me was that the hate seemed to have just disappeared also.

One day, when I was waiting for Katie to arrive for a hair trim, I sat in my big barber chair. I thought about my grandparents and how much I hated them. Although I thought the word hate, I felt no hate. This was strange! I leaned my head back to adjust to this new phenomenon when my eyes rested on a small shelf on the wall near the ceiling. There sat miniature versions of my grandparents. They looked like rag dolls! To make sure I wasn't dreaming, I closed my eyes, then looked back again with one eye. There they were! They looked right comical as their little legs hung over the shelf. The best part was, that they could not move off the shelf nor speak, nor hurt me. This was amazing! Wondering what would happen if I thought about Daddy, I covered my eyes and tried very hard to feel all the old hate. I couldn't, but when I uncovered my eyes, there he sat! Right next to my grandparents, sat a drunken, stuffed doll with his big feet dangling over the shelf. This was fun! Before Katie arrived, a whole bunch of people were sitting on my shelf.

As I took special care of Katie's beautiful blonde curls, I decided not to tell anyone about my imaginary shelf. Goodness! They might think I was a witch. I knew better. God was just helping a child to get rid of destructive feelings, which weighed her down into a murky cesspool. My heart felt light; my voice had a lilt. I felt as free as Black Beauty when he was rescued from his abusers. "Thank you, God, for making yourself known to me. I am so thrilled to know, for sure, that you are really there."

# FORTY-FIVE

Mr. Thigpen was our assistant superintendent. I didn't know him very well. His duty, I supposed, was to assist Mr. Cox. The only time I ever saw him was in church. Tall, lean and blonde, Mr. Thigpen was a nice looking man, all except for his eyes. He had cold, mean, pale blue eyes. I didn't trust him, but I didn't believe the rumor about him either. A few months earlier, Jimmy had been shipped away for accusing Mr. Thigpen of doing unnatural things to him.

There was little communication between the girls and boys sides of the campus; sometimes however, if a rumor started, continued, then persisted in raising its ugly head, the real story gradually became known to everyone.

This was true in the case of Mr. Thigpen. The rumor continued to grow, and another of our boys was shipped away for making a similar accusation.

When girls become curious, they ask questions. The rumor had floated about so long that I was not only curious; I was also concerned for my brothers. I asked Harley, Billy, and several of the boys if they knew anything that would shed light on Mr. Thigpen's alleged behavior. They all denied any first-hand knowledge.

I suppose that I could have asked Columbus, but the information may have come with some obligation. So I sought out my friend, Tommy, who was one of our big boys. He was fourteen.

"You have to tell me the truth, Tommy. I am concerned for my little brothers." I implored.

"Okay, but you have to promise not to tell anyone that I told you this," he answered.

"I won't say a word," I promised.

"Well, if you do tell, you will mess up our plan." said Tommy.

"I said I won't tell, and I mean it," I reassured him.

"Well, all the rumors are true," he began. "He has even gotten after me twice! I'm lucky I'm older and can run fast, but you know that little red-haired guy, Bobby? Thigpen corners him all the time, and Bobby is too small to do anything about it."

"Has he been after either of my brothers? I interrupted.

"Not that I know of, but you don't have to worry because me and some other guys have made up a plan," he said with confidence.

"What kind of a plan?" I asked.

"It's simple; we are going to borrow a camera and set a trap for Mr. Thigpen. Mr. Cox doesn't believe what's going on, but he'll believe it when he sees the pictures."

After much pleading, I convinced Tommy that the boys should set the trap as a last resort. I had so much faith in Mr. Cox, I believed that he would listen to Tommy and the other boys if they went together as a large group.

Mr. Cox not only listened to them. Mr. Cox took swift action and dismissed Mr. Thigpen. He was replaced with one of the finest, most lovable gentlemen I have ever met.

Mr. Hobson Shirey, the new assistant superintendent, was extremely energetic. He seemed to be everywhere all at once. A humorous nature and a twinkle in his eyes, made it hard for the children to keep their unwritten code! "Stick together no matter what, and never, ever, trust those who are in charge."

One evening, Mr. Shirey had supper at our cottage. He told us that our campus needed the beautiful sound of children harmonizing. We had no idea of what he was talking about. He explained it in his own way. "Well, I think you're doing too much work and too little singing! All of you who are interested, show up at the auditorium tomorrow, after school. I'll take care of you chores."

Nearly every girl on campus showed up at the auditorium, which was part of the administration building. Some of the girls came only to avoid chores. I was there because of my true love for music; I wanted to sing!

Mr. Shirey seemed really sincere and excited as he outlined his plan for our chorus. "With some work, you will sound like angels. Somehow, I will get a bus and take you to sing at churches around the state." This was sounding better and better! Except for vacation time, we children never left campus.

Mr. Shirey kept his word, doing more than he had promised. We sang happy songs and inspirational songs like "When you walk through a storm, keep you head up high and don't be afraid of the dark". All the kids at the orphanage had certainly had their share of storms or problems. Encouraging songs like this seemed to say, "It's okay, be brave! You'll get through it."

It's a funny thing about happiness; it comes to you gradually while you're busy doing something you enjoy. We girls, influenced by Mr. Shirey's positive example, took on a far happier attitude. A desire that had lived within me since the first grade, was finally achieved. I sang lead in a girls trio, and was even encouraged and allowed to perform solos.

I no longer knew that hateful, mean girl I used to be. My heart sang, flourishing under the guidance of Mimi Fern, Mr. Cox and now, Mr. Shirey.

# FORTY-SIX

Each boy and girl at the home had his or her own clothing people, as they were called. In order to help the orphanage, different churches from around the state volunteered to clothe an assigned child until the child graduated or left the Home. There was no changing. Once your name was assigned, it became a permanent situation unless the clothing people resigned. Consequently, some of the children were better dressed than others.

My clothing people were from a small, rural, poor church that could not have had more than fifty members. The clothing they sent me was used and often times, too mature for a young girl. I would like to have had pretty new dresses, but somehow, it didn't matter. I was grateful that these people cared enough to share with me what they could.

Just after school was out, I had a letter from Mrs. Madaris. She was the person put in charge of my clothing needs by her church. She informed me that her house had burned and that she was moving to Selma. The bottom line was, that her little country church could no longer sponsor me. "But don't you worry," she wrote. "I will find another church and ask them to sponsor you."

In less than a month, I had another letter from Mrs. Madaris. She explained to me that a new church was being formed in Selma. They had no building, no preacher but they already had twelve members. Not only had these twelve members agreed to sponsor me, they were requesting me for my vacation time. Glory, hallelujah! This vacation was bound to be an improvement over the year before.

Vacation was an exciting time. Every girl in my cottage had her clothes pressed and in the suit case two weeks ahead of time.

On the appointed day, we were awake, had breakfast and cleaned up the dishes in record time. We put into place our need for speed routine. One girl washed, another girl rinsed, still another girl dried the dish then pitched it to waiting hands that quickly shoved it into the cabinet. It was during the pitching that a plate crashed to the floor, shattering into many pieces. One of the pieces landed and stuck right on the front of my ankle. It was a curious feeling, as I yanked it from the main artery, leading to the foot. As soon as I pulled it out, blood started spurting like a geyser.

It was a good thing that Mrs. Madaris drove down to get me instead of sending a bus ticket. Getting stitched up would have caused me to miss the bus.

For a vacation that didn't start off too well, it certainly turned out great. Mrs. Madaris had nine children with only one left at home, a son, who was fourteen years old. I was now thirteen. Our ages were not the only thing Donald and I had in common. We went to movies, went swimming, rode bicycles and stayed up late every night watching scary movies. Donald could play the piano really well. He played and I sang. On Sunday, Donald and I were invited to perform for the church that sponsored me. My first solo for them was entitled, I'm a Child of The King. I had never felt so free! The rigorous routine of the orphanage was far, far away.

On Thursday, before I had to leave on Saturday, Mrs. Madaris announced, "You can't play with Donald today, it's time for you to go shopping!"

Shopping! I just knew I might explode! Feeling no jeopardy or fear of judgment from Mrs. Madaris, I felt it was okay to show my ignorance. "I've never been shopping, how do you do it?" I asked.

Mrs. Madaris laughed. "Oh, you will find it natural enough, I imagine. The hardest part will be to stop shopping."

Belk's department store was like a fairy land and I was the greedy princess who danced about grabbing everything and anything in sight. Loud sounds of giggling eruptions came from my mouth, penetrating every room in the store. I was having a ball, but Mrs. Madaris looked right haggard after the first hour. She quietly suggested that we go to the dressing room to try on several dresses that I was clutching. My excited chatter continued in the dressing room. Mrs. Madaris, who had the patience of Job, finally got a word in edgewise.

"I can see that you really don't know how to shop, so it is up to me to teach you. First, you have to know that we're on a budget."

Before she could continue, I quickly interrupted, "What's a budget?"

Mrs. Madaris smiled, "That's the amount of money we have to spend. We have two hundred dollars; we can't go over that amount."

Without thinking I exclaimed, "You mean to spend that much money on me?"

"Yes," she said, "but remember these clothes have to last you nearly a year, so we have to calm down and use good sense. All these dresses are church dresses, but you also need school dresses, pajamas, underwear and shoes. Let me make a suggestion; let's just start over. We'll go back out there, look at everything in your size, then try on just the things you like best."

Mrs. Madaris was right. Not only had I made a spectacle of myself but I had not used good judgment. Following her lead, I became pretty good at that shopping, even checking price tags to help keep us within budget.

What turned out to be the most exciting day of my life must have been the most harrowing for Mrs. Madaris. The instant we got home, she slumped to her chair and put her feet up. I unpacked all my treasures, modeling all of my dresses for Donald.

Two weeks of fun made it a really sad, hard thing to go back to the orphanage. Two weeks of freedom made it ten times as hard to buckle down, doing everything, at a planned time. I didn't like this, but I did understand that it was a necessity. However, I often times found myself daydreaming about living with Donald, so that every minute of my day would not be scheduled.

# FORTY-SEVEN

The eighth grade marked the beginning of my ambitions stage. I had decided to make something of myself. Just what that something was, hung over me like a cape that was four sizes too large. I had no idea how to be something, but I thought it was worth trying.

More than ever I loved my job of doing hair for the girls, making straight A's for Mr. Cox and singing for Mr. Shirey. Just for myself I skated and collected my Nifty coupons, knowing that one day I would win that shiny, red bicycle. I also took some pride in my bank account. Receiving only fifteen cents allowance per week made it difficult to accumulate very much. Since the sixth grade I had saved a penny, a nickel, sometimes even a whole dime, in my school's banking program. In two years, I had saved $7.43.

One Sunday afternoon, Mimi Fern asked me if I would show a group of visitors around the campus. Since this was my skating time, I wanted to decline. When she told me that Mr. Cox had requested me, of course I had to do it. I did my duty, touring the group all around. When it was concluded, one lady in the group thanked me for my time, and handed me a dollar bill. I was stunned! A whole dollar! I mumbled some kind of thank you and good bye to the group, then ran all the way to Mr. Cox's office. Showing him my new found fortune, I asked, "Do I get to keep it?"

Mr. Cox smiled. "Of course you may. You earned it."

Seeing my chance to make my bank account grow faster than a nickel per week, I pressed Mr. Cox, "Could I show visitors around some more?"

Mr. Cox really looked pleased. "Well," he said, "showing visitors around is strictly volunteer, and, since most of the kids don't want to do it, and, since you've been staying out of trouble . . ." Mr. Cox was playing with me and I knew it. He continued, "Considering you have been making straight A' s . . . I think the answer is yes." Oh, boy! Oh, boy! I knew my face must be smiling. "But, now Mildred, don't always expect a tip; sometimes they don't give one," cautioned Mr. Cox.

I went back to my cottage daydreaming about how rich I was going to be. Sure enough, in a few months time, my bank account had grown to forty-six dollars and eighty-five cents counting interest from the bank. Mr. Cox was right; sometimes the visitors did not give me a tip. Sometimes they gave me a quarter which I gratefully accepted. Most of the time they gave me a dollar, but occasionally I received five whole dollars! One lady, a Mrs. Stallworth, gave me a ten dollar bill, with a promise to come back soon for another tour! Wow! I couldn't believe so many people would give good money just to see an orphanage! On the weekends (that's when they always came) I kept a close watch on the circle in front of the administration building. I was standing on the steps, waiting with a smiling face, before they could get out of the car.

One Sunday afternoon, during campus hour, Winnah and I sat on the grassy lawn talking about different things. She told me how her matron had been generally mistreating her and, that the day before she had slapped her.

"What did you do?" I asked Winnah.

"Nothing," she said. " I just told her that my own mother did not slap me and that she wouldn't do it again. I don't understand," Winnah continued. "I work so hard taking care of the babies. Five and six year olds are really messy and I do most of the cleaning up. I guess she just doesn't like me." Winnah paused as if thinking. "You know the worst part? My clothing people sent me the ugliest Easter dress you've ever seen. It's a brownish color and three sizes too big. It hangs on me like a potato sack. I don't mind used, but the woman who wore this dress must have worn it for eighty years before she died of old age. I'd rather die myself than have to wear it."

I had a big idea formulating. "You don't have to wear it," I injected.

Winnah usually knew when I was up to something but today she was too upset to notice me or hear me. "I guess I just have to wear it. That's just the way it is."

To get her attention, I laid down on the ground and put my head on Winnah's lap. I looked up at her and said, "Our mother used to say that when she knew there was nothing she could do. But we can do something! We can buy you a dress because I have money!" I exclaimed with an impish grin.

"Where did you get money?" Winnah asked.

"Well, I get tips for showing visitors around. Plus, I've been saving my allowance while I bummed chewing gum off you. Come to think of it, I probably owe you enough in chewing gum to buy a dress!"

Winnah recovered quickly. Returning to her old self, she suggested, "Do your chores quickly this Saturday and get permission to go up town. I'll do the same and we'll meet right down there on the sidewalk."

Winnah's plan worked perfectly. We did get her a beautiful new Easter dress and there was not one thing her matron could do about it.

From this experience I learned a valuable lesson. I came to a vague notion that being dependent on someone gave them power over you. If they were a bad person, like Winnah's matron, they would most assuredly exercise that power to your detriment. I decided that we all needed to hurry up with this growing up and take charge of ourselves.

Thank goodness Winnah did not have to stay in that cottage much longer. She was moved to our small infirmary where duties included assisting Mrs. Tindal, our on campus nurse. Winnah was great at taking care of sick folks; I thought she might become a doctor. Best of all, Winnah and Mrs. Tindal liked each other. Unless some of the kids were sick, Winnah had more freedom and time to study since she and Mrs. Tindal were the only residents of the infirmary.

The orphanage had a small swimming pool that was directly across the road from the infirmary. It opened soon after school was out with cottages rotating swim time. My cottage was assigned Monday, Wednesday and Friday at three o'clock. I loved to swim and dive off the spring board, pretending to be a beautiful swan.

I found myself in deep water, in more than one way, when I developed a painful cramp in my right leg. I kicked as hard I as I could, to try to get it out. I must have kicked too hard as a peculiar thing happened. My leg drew backward. It would not straighten or move, just about immobilizing me. The pain from my leg was excruciating.

The more I yelled for help, the more my friends laughed. I was bobbing up and down in danger of drowning. Everyone thought I was just showing off.

Winnah did not think I was pretending; she filtered my cry for help from all the other voices. From the infirmary, across the road, past the shallow end and all the way to the deep end of the pool, Winnah was there, dragging me from the pool to safety. Some of the girls taunted Winnah as she carried me on her back to the infirmary. "She's just acting; she's not hurt!" Winnah knew better. "This is my little sister! I will decide when she is pretending." Winnah retorted.

The infirmary was not equipped to treat injuries as serious as mine. It was discovered that I had broken a ligament, which accounted for the enormous pain. The injury required that I be taken to the hospital in town, where my leg was encased in a cast, and I was told that I would have to wear it for about five weeks.

"Well, at least the cast will be off in time for vacation," I thought.

Mrs. Madaris was right on time picking me up for vacation. Wonderful! She brought Donald! Although we had not seen each other for a year, it was as though we had never been apart. We loved each other. Donald was like my brother.

Mrs. Madaris told me that the church had arranged for me to go to camp for the first week, and then spend the second week with the Madaris family.

"Is Donald going?" I asked.

"No, this is a girl's camp" replied Mrs. Madaris.

"I might not like camp. I might rather stay with Donald!"

"I promise, you will like it or I will come and get you," assured Mrs. Madaris. "By the way, if you like, you can call me Mama Madaris."

I did not respond. Was Mrs. Madaris trying to take the place of my mother? Although I had gradually developed a deep caring for Mrs. Madaris, she could not be my mother. No one would ever fill that spot in my heart. I became very quiet as I thought about the offer that had been made to me. Wondering if she might be offended if I did not accept, I thought about all her attributes.

Mrs. Madaris was, I believed, the kindest, most gentle person I had ever known. Her attitude towards me, and all children, was always room for one more, although her income was very limited. It does not take wealth to be a very giving person if you give of yourself. Mrs. Madaris gave me her non-critical, caring self. Mrs. Madaris never referred to me as that poor little orphan girl nor bragged about what all she had done for me. Her introduction of me to others allowed me to be a special person. "This is one of my girls," she would say, or "This is our little girl, Mildred."

I decided that I should give Mrs. Madaris something in return but I had no gifts to give.

When we arrived at her home in Selma, I asked, "How would it be if I called you Mama 'daris?"

A quick laugh and a special hug made me know that my gift had been accepted. Mama 'daris would not take the place of my mother, but she was to become a guiding light, a firm foundation, that helped me to know who I was, and where I was going.

That Sunday, I was an honored guest at my clothing sponsor's new church. I could hardly believe it! Their membership had grown to three hundred or more and they had built a small brick church in just a year. They called it Elkdale Baptist Church. The preacher, Dr. Kirkland, and his wife were so young and friendly that I felt right at home, more than willing to sing for the church whenever called upon.

Monday morning, I was off to the camp. I did not think of this as a new adventure, but just a way to please Mama 'daris. I wanted to stay with Donald. As it turned out, though, I found it to be loads of fun. There was canoeing, crafts, swimming, hiking and just being part of the great outdoors. My leg sometimes hurt but I knew it was slowly getting better.

On Wednesday evening, we had what they called a lakeside service. It was wonderful! Lots of singing, and prayers for peace in the world, had my complete attention. I wanted it to never end, although my leg was hurting and I felt like I could no longer stand. Quietly, I folded my right leg behind me to sit down on the ground. An awful pain shot through my knee and I heard a very unpleasant cracking sound from my leg. The ligament had given way again and I had broken my leg! I knew it. My first thought should have been to get to a doctor. Instead, my only thought was how to hide my injury until my vacation time was up. There was no way I would give up my vacation for a broken leg.

The service came to an end with the burning of a cross on the far side of the lake. It was very moving. To my dismay, I could not move to carry myself up the hill, back to my cabin. A good-looking, muscular lifeguard named James, carried me all the way, insisting that it was no trouble. I insisted that my leg was only sprained, that it would be better in the morning.

The next morning, as I lowered myself from the top bunk, I collapsed to the floor. My leg was huge! Still, I pretended to the camp folks that I was fine. My pretense continued through the next week that I spent with the Madaris family. A little pain was not about to ruin my time away from the orphanage! Of course, I could not teach Donald gymnastics, nor could we ride bikes. But the freedom . . . oh, the freedom, was worth all the pain.

When Mama 'daris checked me into the orphanage, I said to Mr. Cox, "Well, you can take me to the hospital now; my leg is broken."

Mama ‘daris just about fainted from embarrassment and concern. “Little girl, if you knew your leg was broken, why did you let me take you shopping?”

I, with honesty replied, “Because I wanted to go shopping.”

My leg was indeed broken. I had to lie on my back, with my leg hoisted in the air, for two whole weeks before the swelling went down. Then the doctor put my leg in a cast and gave me wooden crutches with which to walk.

I don’t know if my own personal neglect, malnutrition during my early years, or what, but my leg would not heal. After six weeks of wearing a cast, Dr. Edge told me that my leg had not even begun to knit back together. I had to start calcium shots.

Every Friday after school, come rain or shine, I walked to Edge’s Clinic, books balanced on the handles of my crutches. I did my homework while I waited to see Dr. Edge.

After several such visits, I began to notice that I was always the last patient to be seen by Dr. Edge. I began to realize, that even those who arrived an hour after I did, were seen before me. I knew what was going on, but I also knew there was little I could do about it, except whine to Mr. Cox. I didn’t want to cause a problem for Mr. Cox, so each Friday, after struggling to get there, I waited . . . and waited for a calcium shot that was given with a dull needle, guaranteed to keep my arms black and blue. I knew I wasn’t being given good treatment. I didn’t see why Winnah could not give my calcium shots at our campus infirmary. She could give much better shots than Dr. Edge.

Often times, I had to walk back to my cottage after dark. The route from the hospital, Edge’s Clinic, carried me through an old part of town where many of the houses, unoccupied and run down, gave off a ghostly aura. Most of the store buildings were closed and dark. Street lights were dim, if there were any, and danger seemed to hide around each approaching corner. I was always relieved and elated when I reached Elm Street. There I felt safe. It was only one more mile to home.

Two years later, I was still taking calcium shots, mobilizing by use of crutches and having my leg x-rayed several times every week. Dr. Edge had grown weary of my leg not healing. He thought of a solution - amputate!

Now, I had put up with a great deal of bad treatment for two years and I decided enough was enough! I sure wished Winnah was here to help me, but she wasn't, so I had to stand up for myself.

"No," I said. "You will not cut off my leg! You will take this cast off my leg and I will swim."

Dr. Edge said, "The bone has not healed and the muscles have withered from lack of use. If you put any weight on that leg, the bone will splinter into several pieces. The pain will be indescribable."

My stubborn nature took over. "Fine," I said, "if that happens then you can cut it off. Meanwhile, I will use my crutches, and let my leg float in the shallow end of the pool." The pool had just opened for summer.

Dr. Edge seemed god-like. I couldn't believe that I had stood up to him. I only believed it when they cranked up the saw, cut off my cast and said, "Okay, you can go home."

The mile and a half to the orphanage was so scary. What if I fell? What if I accidentally put weight on my leg? It was so small, half the size of my left leg! It felt so unprotected without the cast!

All this wondering was too much to think about. I decided not to think about it; just keep my leg as long as I could.

Perhaps it was a prayed for miracle. Perhaps it was the sunshine that helped me absorb all that calcium. I don't know. I just know that by summers end, Dr. Edge announced, "Your bone has almost healed. You might start putting a little weight on it. Just a little, mind you. Maybe the muscles will start to plump up."

I had won! With no one to stand up for me, but myself, I had kept my leg. "Thank you, God, for giving me a stubborn nature."

# FORTY-EIGHT

Much had happened during the last two years, while my leg was healing. I had kept my grades up and become a member of the Beta Club. Cutting a head of hair now took minutes, when it used to take an hour. I had managed to grow taller than Mama 'daris. She was still about four feet eleven inches and I was now five feet one inch. Due to my age, I had been moved to a new cottage where there were only six girls to a room.

Mrs. Stallworth, the lady who had given me a $10.00 tip for showing her around, had become a frequent visitor to the orphanage. In my heart, I felt that she was coming just to see me. What a compliment! Mrs. Stallworth was a handsome woman. She was tall, richly dressed, with makeup and hair perfectly done. I knew she had to be wealthy because she continued to give me ten dollars every time she came, which was at least twice a year. During the latter part of February, Mrs. Stallworth showed up with two boxes that were meticulously wrapped and tied with bright colored ribbons.

"For me?" I asked.

"Yes," she answered. "I hear that you're having a birthday next month so I wanted to bring you a little something."

Words could never describe how special I felt. Inside the smallest gift was luscious chocolate candy. The larger present was a beautiful, blue Sunday dress. I hugged Mrs. Stallworth and thanked her profusely.

"What will you do at your birthday party?" Mrs. Stallworth asked.

"Oh, we don't have parties; there are too many of us to have parties," I reasoned.

"Then we'll just have to throw a party for you at my house. I'll get permission from Mr. Cox," Mrs. Stallworth stated. "That would be wonderful, but I think Mr. Cox will say "NO"; the only time any of us get to leave this place is in August. That's our two week vacation," I informed Mrs. Stallworth.

"Well, we shall see about that," Mrs. Stallworth said with a very self confident tone.

Mrs. Stallworth's positive manner must have paid off as I was the first kid ever to leave on a weekend trip. Mrs. Stallworth came for me and took me to her home some forty miles away. It was a small town, with a rich history, as evidenced by the well kept ante-bellum homes. Mrs. Stallworth owned one of these mansions, as well as, the only clothing store in town.

Upon arrival, Mrs. Stallworth gave me a grand tour of her home, pointing out various antiques and explaining to me their value. I had no reason to doubt her word. I did wonder if I should give her a tip for the tour.

"Now, I think you should go up to your room, unpack and rest. I want you to look your prettiest for the party this afternoon. You will find a new birthday dress in the closet." As I started up the winding staircase, Mrs. Stallworth added, "The maid will be up soon to draw your bath."

My fifteenth birthday party was the finest money could buy. It was hard for me to believe that so many strangers would show up with beautifully wrapped gifts for a girl they had never before met.

What was harder to believe was the manner in which Mrs. Stallworth introduced me to her guests, "This is my little orphan girl whom I've told you so much about." Then she told them all the wonderful things she had done for me, as well as the orphanage. All the guests treated me with great kindness and sympathy. I was glad for the party to finally end.

The next day was Sunday. Mrs. Stallworth again dressed me up in the finest dress from her store to show me off to her church members. I was beginning to feel like a prize pig in a county fair! Before his sermon, the preacher announced that a poor little orphan girl was attending. He asked me to stand for all to view. Then the deacons passed the plate for a special offering to be sent to the orphanage. This was good! I knew Mr. Cox needed all the money he could get just to feed all the children.

After the service, most of the members got in line to meet me. Mrs. Stallworth was the center of attention as she continued to pontificate, describing all the generous and kind things she had done for me. In the eyes of the people, I could see the admiration for Mrs. Stallworth and the great pity for me. I wanted to scream, "Don't feel sorry for me; I'm special! I am a survivor. I am my Mother's daughter!" But, I said nothing. I was too embarrassed and confused to say anything.

On the way back to the home, I thought about all the wonderful birthday gifts I had received. I decided that I would rather not have them. To be pitied and belittled was too high a price for any number of gifts.

It took several months, and another visit from Mrs. Stallworth, before I could forgive her. I never told her how she had hurt me, for in my heart I didn't believe she intended to. I decided that she was just using me to get some sorely needed attention. Still, the realization that I had been used, caused me to resolve that there would be no more birthday parties, nor visits to her home.

In early August, Mr. Cox informed me that, as usual, the Madaris family had requested me for vacation. Mrs. Stallworth had also requested me.

"This is a problem," stated Mr. Cox. "You know that Mrs. Stallworth has donated quite a sum of money to our home, don't you?"

"Yes sir; she has also given me money and gifts. I really care about Mrs. Stallworth and I like being around her when it is just the two of us. I just don't like her when she's with her friends," I confessed.

"I see," said Mr. Cox. "And how is it when you're with the Madaris family?" he asked. "It feels good," I responded. "Mama 'daris hugs me and buys me apples. She lets me stay up late and teaches me things like budgeting. Donald plays with me and is teaching me to play the piano. Mama 'daris has grown up children too, that teach me things like water skiing and fishing."

There was a long pause. I broke the silence with a question. "Mr. Cox, would you just tell Mrs. Stallworth that clothing people always have first choice?"

Mr. Cox smiled and said something I never expected. "Mildred, every day you are growing taller, prettier and wiser. You are learning to reason, making the right choices. A pretty girl who uses her mind can go far." I left Mr. Cox's office dancing on air. Go far! That's exactly what I wanted to do. . . go far!

My vacation was the best ever. Donald and I found a sort of beach. A paved road used to be there, but the water had long since washed it out. Young car owners came there to wash their cars.

Donald and I sat on the pavement, letting the water run over our legs, day dreaming about the time when we, too, would own a car. I told Donald that having a car seemed so far off, that right now, I would be extremely happy if I could just have a bicycle.

"Is there any way you can get one?" asked Donald. I told Donald about my boxes and boxes of Nifty coupons that I had been saving for nearly four years.

"Why don't you send them in? he asked.

"I've started to several times, but I've always been afraid that I wouldn't have the most. The girl and boy that sends in the most are the ones who win," I answered.

"Well," Donald reasoned, "when you're all grown up, you won't need a bike, so you may as well take a chance on getting it while you're still a kid."

It was a little embarrassing when Mama 'daris took me on my annual shopping spree. She looked up at me, stating with a certainty, "Little girl, fifteen and a half years of age is too old to be running around without a bra. This year, we have to add one more item to your shopping list."

I thought I would die when the clerk said she had to size me. What size? I had just lately begun to sprout! Down deep, though, I was glad of Mama 'daris's decision. All my friends were already having periods and filling out big bras. I wasn't. Maybe a bra would make me feel more normal, no matter how embarrassing it was to get one.

My wonderful vacation was soon over and I was back at the children's home. The rigorous routine of school and work took over my life. Still, I thought about my shiny, new, red bike and what Donald had said. So, with great fear of not having the most, I counted my thousands of Nifty coupons, packaging them neatly. Mr. Cox's secretary helped me decide the correct postage for my prized box, and I mailed it with a prayer and a great hope. Now, all I could do was wait. Down deep, I felt that I had a good chance of winning. After all, how many girls in the country had her own beauty shop? How many girls in the country received no pay except that of Nifty coupons for doing hair ? Probably none. Therefore, I decided that I would most likely win!

# FORTY-NINE

I had not seen hide nor hair of Harley lately. We hadn't walked to school nor talked at campus hour in weeks. When I did see him it was at a distance. Upon seeing me, he would walk in the opposite direction. Finally I cornered him at church, demanding to know what was going on.

"I can't tell you," he said.

"I know that you were fine until last month, about the time you were assigned to barn duty," I said.

"I know," Harley agreed.

"But, you like getting up early, feeding hogs and gathering eggs." I reasoned.

"I know," he repeated.

"Well, you told me, yourself, that you like milking the cows. So what is the problem?" I insisted.

Harley examined his feet, and fixed his gaze on something far off.

"I do like all that; I just can't stand to hear Columbus run his ugly mouth."

Harley, at last began to respond, so I prompted him with another question.

"Was he assigned to work with you?"

"Yea," he continued, "and you know how I hate his guts. I try not to be around him, or talk to him. The problem is . . . he talks to me."

"Did he say something that made you mad?" I asked.

"He sure did! He said he f___ed you. He kept on saying it, over and over 'til I couldn't take it no more, so I hit him in the head with a shovel."

"Did he hit you back?" I asked.

"No. He fell in a big pile of cow shit that we had scraped up. I started to hit him again, but I didn't 'cause he wasn't moving," was his reply.

"What did you do next?" I prompted.

"Well, when I saw blood running from his head into the cow manure, I thought he was dead. I went around to the other side of the barn and waited for somebody to find him." Harley admitted.

"Did any one find him?" I asked.

"No. Nobody came by, so after a long time I slipped around to check on him. And there he was, shoveling that shit, like nothing had ever happened. I started working too, but I kept my distance." Harley continued.

Relived, I asked, "Was that the end of it?"

"No, but Columbus was real quiet, so I thought it was all over. Columbus didn't say anything for a long time, so after a while I, sort of, dropped my guard. As soon as I turned my back, Columbus jumped me."

"But, Columbus is twice your size!" I exclaimed

Harley replied, "I know. That's why it was so easy for him to pin my arms behind me, push me, face down, in that pile of cow manure and roll me around in it until I was covered from head to toe. Through the whole thing, he never said a word, and when he was finished he just walked off."

"Then, what did you do?" I again prompted.

"The only thing I could do. I got myself out of that slippery mess and headed for the pond. I washed myself off as best I could and went back to finish my job."

"Have you talked to Columbus since then?" I queried.

"No! . . .And I'm not about to . . . . did he really screw you?"

At this point I was laughing uncontrollably. "Harley, I won't even let Columbus hold my hand! I can't believe you fell for such a lie! Columbus was just trying to rile you," I said, still laughing.

But Harley was dead serious as he blurted out loudly, "He didn't rile me. He made me so damn mad I wanted to kill that so and so."

# FIFTY

Baseball had become a tradition at the children's home. Every Sunday, during campus hour, any kid could get in the game. Sometimes there was as many as thirty kids to each team. Age, size or sex made no difference. No one was ever turned away. If a kid owned a baseball or a bat, that kid was special and was given priority status in the batting line up. The player lucky enough to own a glove was also special and automatically given a position of infielder or catcher.

Billy, now eleven years of age, had become very interested in baseball, but with no ownership in a ball, bat or glove he was doomed to the outfield, along with thirty or so other kids. The possibility of getting a turn at bat was almost zero, since the game lasted only one hour. Billy longed for a glove so that he could get a chance at bat. I did not know how much Billy dreamed of a baseball glove until Harley told me. He also told me how he would like to play football, but that he had no ball to practice with.

I told Harley about my dream to have my own bicycle, that my dream might come true. "Don't give up," I told him, "If you want something so much, it's bound to happen sooner or later. I just hope you and Billy don't have to wait as long as I have had to wait."

As time went by, I thought more and more about my brothers' desires for a football and baseball glove. I thought about buying them, but I didn't have enough money.

Urgent desires called for urgent action, so I went to Mr. Cox. As Christmas wasn't far off, I thought Santa Clause might pitch in to make two boys extremely happy.

"I'm sorry Mildred," Mr. Cox responded to my request, "The Home doesn't have that kind of money. I wish we could give such fine gifts, but we can't."

So, that was that. Now, I knew it was up to me to figure out a way for my brothers to have a football and glove. "Maybe Mrs. Stallworth will come back," I thought, "with just six dollars, along with my bank account, I would have enough by Christmas. Weeks went by and I had only added two dollars and thirty six cents to my bank account. Not enough!

No matter how much I smiled - no matter how good a job I did showing visitors around, they gave few tips, usually nothing - sometimes a quarter.

A few days before Christmas I was summoned to the office. There I was shown a huge cardboard box with my name on it. My heart did flip-flops in anticipation as I pried open one side of the box and peered in.

There it was! The deep red, shiny hunk of metal that had been the object of my dreams for the last four years. "I WON! I WON!," I exclaimed. At last, I had won. Now I would fly like the wind, enjoying the envy and admiration of every kid on the campus. "I sure hope Harley and Billy don't have to wait four years to get their football and glove," I thought as I eagerly began pulling my brand new bike from it's carton.

Suddenly, I slumped to the floor, my eyes intent upon the cardboard container. I knew that bike would never be ridden by me. Soon to be sixteen, I had gotten too old to place such importance on a bike. The one thing I had wanted so much and waited so long to get, suddenly meant so little. What I really wanted most was a football and a baseball glove.

Permission to go up town was given to my friend Mary and me. With a great deal of effort, she and I managed to carry, pull and drag my prize the mile or so to the Western Auto store. The store owner, Mr. Hollis, was my Sunday School teacher's husband. I asked him if he would like to buy my bike. "I don't buy bikes," he said, " I sell them." Determined not to leave without what I came for, I explained to Mr. Hollis that I did not want money, I just wanted an even trade - my brand new bike for one football and one baseball glove.

I had no idea if it was an even exchange. All I knew was, that my brothers had their Christmas wishes, and I had the pleasure of making them come true.

# FIFTY-ONE

Spring came and I reached the important age of sixteen. Most of the girls looked forward to this birthday because they were allowed to go on a date once a month. Strict, emphatic rules applied to dating. Rule number one was never to ride in a car with a boy. Walk only to one place, the local theater. Never leave before six o'clock on Saturday night only and always be home by ten o'clock or else. That or else meant extra chores and giving up three dates, one date for the next three months. Some of the girls complained that they had to leave before the movie was over in order to arrive home by ten o'clock.

I had no need to worry about the rules, as not one boy, except Columbus, would ask me out. Was something wrong with me? Did I have bad breath, body odor, or some ugly malady that plagued young girls? There was nothing to do but to ask my friend Herman, a small, dark skinned town boy.

"What's wrong with me?" I asked him.

"Nothing," he answered.

"Then tell me why no one will ask me for a date?" I insisted.

"I can't tell you," Herman evaded.

"Then, you do know why, and you're going to tell me." I insisted.

"If I do, he will kill me," he exclaimed.

"If you don't tell me, I will kill you, Herman!" I declared.

"Well, you'd better not say I told you, unless you want me dead. Columbus has dared any one to ask you. He said that he would kill any boy that looked at you!," Herman whispered confidentially, cupping his hands around his mouth.

I knew Herman was telling me the truth.

I didn't blame the boys for being afraid of Columbus. He was extremely explosive. What Columbus could not understand was that I had grown to think of him as a brother. Most of the kids at the Home had a brotherly and sisterly attitude towards each other.

Two of my friends would not adhere to the dating rules. Nearly every Friday night they sneaked out of the house to meet boys. They later told the rest of us girls about their sexual experiences, leaving out no details. I didn't understand. Both girls had been raped for years by their father or step father before coming to the orphanage. It seemed to me that they should be the first to run from any male. Instead, they sought after the sexual activity, even enjoyed it. I wondered if they were not re-enacting their childhood abuse.

I knew one thing for sure. No matter how exciting their adventures seemed, this misconduct was not for me. I had no intentions of self-destructing. I wanted to be something.

Being sixteen was scary for several reasons. My being sixteen meant Winnah had reached age eighteen. It was the rule. She had to leave the orphanage forever. Although we had little contact on a day to day basis, I, at least, knew where she was. Now, she was leaving. Campus hour would never be the same.

Although I was sad and a little bit mad about Winnah's leaving, I was also very proud of her for growing up to be so smart and beautiful. Her scholastic achievements had netted her a full scholarship at Samford University in Birmingham. Most eighteen year olds did not leave with scholarships. They took jobs or got married. A few worked their own way through college.

Because there was no other choice, I made up my mind to work extra hard, study extra hard for the next two years. Then, I too, would win a scholarship, and join Winnah in college.

Soon after Winnah left, it was decided that all children on campus, sixteen years and under should have their tonsils removed. Great day! That was over one hundred and fifty kids!

My tonsils never hurt; I was never sick! I objected loudly to this unneeded surgery, fearing that it would affect my singing voice. Objections were rarely considered at the Home and this time was no exception.

The wholesale removal of our tonsils began Monday morning. I was one of the first to go under the knife, awakening slowly to a dull hurting in my throat. This was no surprise; I expected it.

What I did not expect was to find a boy, halfway on my bed, fondling my chest! It was Johnny, a town boy, I recognized from school. I tried to yell "Stop," but my voice would not work. I tried to push him away but I was so groggy that I couldn't. Somehow I managed to get my left leg from under the sheet, kicking at anything my foot could hit. Soon I heard him yelp and vaguely sensed that he had left the room. I decided to report him when I was better. Right now, I felt too bad to think about it.

The second time I awoke, I wondered if Johnny's misbehavior had only been a bad dream. It wasn't a dream. I had the evidence in my hand. Johnny had lost his comb during the struggle. I knew that I would never tell a living soul. It would only cause trouble for Mr. Cox because Johnny happened to be the son of a very prominent man in our church.

It was likely that no one would believe me. All that would happen would be that I would lose all hope of a college scholarship. So I kept my mouth shut, leaving the hospital with a sense of relief. Now I could go back to the orphanage where I was safe. It had become my village of refuge.

Ten days later, on Sunday morning, I awoke choking, with blood all over me as well as my bed. I was carried back to the hospital where I was put in a temporary room. A nurse clamped my throat with two metal objects, each a foot long, that made me gag and heave from the stomach.

"Lie on your back and keep still. The doctor will be here soon," the nurse said as she left.

Hours later, I was certain that the nurse had forgotten that I was there. If only I could yell for help! I knew that I might go out of my mind if I didn't quit thinking about my predicament; maybe if I didn't look at the metal tongs I would quit heaving. So I rolled over on my side, letting the blood drip directly to the floor. Good! Now I wasn't gagging so much as the blood was no longer collecting in my throat. There was no choice but to wait so I forced myself to think of other things.

I thought about my wonderful sister Winnah. She would make somebody look after me if she was here. Mr. Cox would, too, if he knew what was happening. Mr. Cox had every reason to believe I was being well cared for. After all, this was a hospital.

I wondered if all patients got poor treatment here or if it was just the orphans. I worried that Mr. Cox had not been able to pay the whole bill for all those tonsillectomies. Maybe that's why I was being ignored. I envisioned myself as being a grown up. I would make lots of money and always pay my bills in full. That way I could demand good treatment.

It was early evening before anyone came to check on me. Dr. Crook smiled at me saying, "I hear we have a problem." If I could have talked I would have replied, "No, sir. The problem is yours. It should weigh heavy on your conscience that you have let me suffer all day." The metal clamps allowed me to say nothing.

As I was wheeled off to surgery I thought of my wonderful mother and her philosophy, "Sometimes there is nothing you can do."

The next day, I was brought back to the infirmary on our campus.

The following Sunday, Mrs. Stallworth came for a visit. Mostly, she did the talking as we walked around campus. Her voice was so refined and pleasant, a truly cultured southern accent. I found myself listening to her pronunciations, hoping that one day I might sound so refined, so knowledgeable and dignified.

Mrs. Stallworth wanted me to come to her home for vacation. I had no intention of visiting her again, because of the way she treated me in front of her friends. On the other hand, I didn't want to hurt her feelings by telling her this truth, so I again claimed that my clothing people in Selma had first priority.

# FIFTY-TWO

That fall, I started my all-important junior year in high school. It was marked by fun things like singing in the adult choir at church, occasionally being loaned out to other churches for solo parts. I even got to sing at our junior-senior prom by promising to leave as soon as my solo was over. Kids from the orphanage were not allowed to go to dances or proms. The fact that I was allowed to go long enough to sing was a real first.

Because of my good grades, Mr. Cox allowed me to take part in the junior / senior play. Landing the leading role made me feel very special. I liked the acting and found that I was pretty good at it, except for the kiss I had to give to the leading man at the end.

What I liked best was hanging around with my classmates, the town kids, and getting to know them better during rehearsals. I had no idea they were so much fun. Bitsey Murphree and Becky Brantly were the comics of the group. Mimi McKinnon was always fresh as a daisy, no matter what the temperature. Marcia Chapman was wise beyond her years. Diane Gibson was a true friend to everyone. Marcia Davis was destined to succeed. Then, there was brilliant Carolyn Stewart, beautiful Eleanor Herlong, and sweet Martha Shiver. I found that the town kids were just regular kids, just like me. I knew then that I would regret the rest of my life not having the opportunity to pal around with them more and know them better. Mrs. Gibson, Diane's mother, being a very persuasive lady, convinced Mr. Cox to allow some of the town girls to spend the night with me after the play. I believe each enjoyed the experience.

My shyness made it difficult to talk to the town boys, even at rehearsal. Mind you, I did take notice of them. How could one not notice the fun loving Dozier twins, the reserved Tom Murphree, the gorgeous Bobby Howard or the all around "good guy" Richard Head.

Cecil Dozier was later to write in my yearbook, "Thanks for the good times we never had." He never knew it, but this statement really touched my heart. It underscored my loss. I was like a bystander, observing this wonderful carefree time, but not fully participating in the fun - and I enjoyed more privileges than most of the home children.

Although most hours in the lives of Home kids were busy and productive, there was still enough time for the mischievous to entertain themselves. One evening, on the way to church, a dozen or so of us girls stopped at the local drug store. By pooling our nickels and dimes, we had just enough money to buy the cheapest bottle of cologne in the whole store. It was TWEED, the most pungent odor I had ever smelled. My friends and I took turns splashing it all over us until the bottle was empty.

We sat together, as a group, in church. Our presence was witnessed by all, as evidenced by the sneezing, coughing and wheezing by the other members of the congregation. The preacher cut his sermon very short, setting a record for the invitational and closing prayer.

When I saw Mr. Cox after church, he gave me a knowing nod followed by this bit of wisdom, "Mildred, moderation is a virtue, and sometimes more is not necessarily better."

That spring, just after my seventeenth birthday, the TWENTY ONE CLUB was having it's annual Miss Troy contest at the local drive-in movie. The TWENTY ONE CLUB was a social club for fine young women of our town. The girls from the Home were not allowed to take part in social doings. Still, I wondered what it would be like to be on stage and be introduced as one of the twenty one girls representing our fair town of Troy.

The thought of sweeping across stage in an evening gown was exciting but the swimsuit part made me cringe. I was now a skinny five foot six with no waist and no hips. Where other girls seemed to curve out, I seemed to hang straight down. I believed that God had gotten mixed up and accidentally given me boy legs. Everyone knew

I had boy legs because I had told them so. It was just as well that I could not be in the contest.

That Friday at school, my friend Diane told me that one of the contestants had come down with the flu.

"It's tradition," she said. "We have to have twenty-one girls. Now, I know you can't win, since you have boy legs and all, but why don't you just fill in for her?"

I was dumbfounded. A girl from the orphanage was being asked to take part in a town social event? "I can't," I mumbled. "Mr. Cox would never give permission."

Diane stood firm. "You just go ahead and borrow an evening gown. My mother will call Mr. Cox."

So that's how I came to be MISS TROY, representing our town. As the key to the city and the dozen red roses were placed in my hands, I wondered how on earth I had won. Perhaps it was because the judges were from out of town. They hadn't heard that I had boy legs.

# FIFTY-THREE

A strange, new couple had been on our campus for several months now. They were the cottage parents to what we called the big boys cottage where Columbus lived. They were an older couple. Mr. McGhee was a former police chief from a nearby town. He bragged that he could get rid of any boy that didn't tow the line. Rumor was, that three of our boys had already been shipped off. The next one in line was probably Columbus. This worried me. I knew that Columbus could not be passive. He could not walk the straight and narrow even if his life depended on it.

Columbus had long since lost his boyhood fat. As he promised he would do, he had turned it all into muscle. Columbus had become a good-looking young man with huge shoulders and a narrow behind. Moreover, he was a talented football player, very valuable as our high school's first-string fullback.

I was surprised that an old guy like Mr. McGhee would dare to tangle with someone like Columbus. After months of goading and verbal pushing, Columbus exploded on Mr. McGhee. Of course, there could be only one real looser and that was Columbus, who had to leave the home forever. Columbus moved in with a family in town, continuing his high school education from off campus.

I told Mr. Cox how upset I was that Columbus had been badgered into leaving, because he was like a brother to me. "Now, what kind of future would he have?" I wondered.

Now Harley had become of great concern to me. I knew, that at age sixteen, he would be moved into Mr. McGhee's cottage. There was no way Harley would take abuse; he would surely get in a fight and be sent away just like Columbus.

"You worry too much, Mildred," replied Mr. Cox. "You know that every child here has to stand on his or her own two feet. Nobody made Columbus explode. Besides, you have no idea how hard it is to get people to work here. To become house-parents, they practically have to give up their whole lives, then work for a very small paycheck. Now, suppose you look after Mildred's business and I will look after the institution's business."

My objections had been heard but not heeded. Three months later Harley was moved to the McGhee cottage.

My senior year at Troy High would have been a very happy time had I not been constantly worried about Harley.

"Mr. McGhee is trying to get to you. Don't let him win," I would say to Harley. "Be like Burt. He survives Mr. McGhee by ignoring him. Burt will have a scholarship when he graduates with me this June. You're smart. You can get a scholarship too, if you can just stay here for just two more years."

I knew my words could not postpone the inevitable as I continued to hear rumors of skirmishes between Harley and Mr. McGhee. It was as though I was holding my breath waiting and dreading the surety of Harley's expulsion.

The Children's Home built a new cottage for junior and senior girls. The bedrooms were designed to house two girls with a bathroom that connected to another bedroom accommodating two girls. This was amazing. I felt like a queen to have a bathroom shared only by three others. And just one roommate! The orphanage must finally be getting rich. Mr. Cox's letter writing must be paying off!

Marie and I chose each other for roommates. Although we had come to the Home the same year, I really didn't know her until we were moved into the same cottage a year and a half before. Marie was beautiful as well as very bright, but there was no competition between us. Although she had experienced a tumultuous childhood, Marie did not feel victimized. I don't believe she felt like an orphan. I know I didn't. I just felt like me. We had much in common as we both possessed a sense of who we were and where we were going. Sharing a room with Marie made my last year at the orphanage extremely special.

My life was good! I had even started dating a wonderful young man who was a senior at Auburn University. Tom was not intimidated by Columbus's threats. Tom did not know Columbus. They had never met.

In 1958, the dating rule of once a month and no riding in cars was still in force. However, we were allowed to sit with our boyfriends in church. They could even walk us home after service, whether noon or evening. It occurred to me that Tom should have found an easier girl to date. After walking me home from church, he had to walk a mile and a half back to the church where his pale yellow 1957 Chevrolet was parked.

# FIFTY-FOUR

One week before graduation, I postponed the night's sleep by thinking about the speech I had been asked to give. I had decided to speak about choices, to challenge my classmates to have happier lives by making the right choices. "How pompous you are," I chided myself. "Not I, nor any of my classmates have any idea of what we would encounter after graduation."

For the first time, I felt a little envious of the town kids. They could choose to stay with their parents if they wanted. In just one week, the very bed that I was then sleeping on would be given to another girl. Seven of us graduating orphans would be given one suitcase and one steam iron each. With this, we were expected to leave the security of the Home and to make our own way in the world.

This was both exciting and frightening! Getting on my own was what I yearned for - now I was afraid. Being sheltered by the orphanage, I was totally ignorant toward the ways of the world. It occurred to me that I had never been to a restaurant, been inside a bank or grocery store. I had never paid a bill nor ridden in a car on a date. Would I know how to act? Would I mess up?

The excitement of getting on my own gradually won over my fears. As I drifted off to sleep, the lyrics to my favorite hymn again played across my mind, I'll Fly Away. I would make my own safe place, not letting fear of the unknown deter me.

Mr. Cox counseled me about my plans, reminding me that my full scholarship to Samford University covered tuition only. I would need to earn money for clothes, toothpaste, food, etc.

By now, I was an accomplished hairdresser but would be unable to get a job with no license. Mr. Cox suggested that I go to cosmetology school in Montgomery. He felt certain that I could acquire my license in time to start college in the fall.

Mr. Cox was correct in his thinking. After trying out at the school, I was awarded free tuition along with a small salary for functioning as assistant instructor. This provided me with enough money to pay my room at the YWCA and buy two cheap meals per day. This was fine. My two good feet would act as transportation.

An ugly pink, the YWCA left a lot to be desired, primarily due to its occupants. I had never seen girls like these. Big, boyish, and rough looking, they frightened me. Thank goodness I only slept there. Not being air-conditioned, it was mighty hot, but no matter the temperature, I bolted my door every night.

The duties of my Selma clothing people ceased when I graduated high school. By no means did this end my relationship with the Madaris family. Love is not a relationship that ends abruptly.

During my one week off from cosmetology school, Margaret, one of Mama 'daris's daughters invited me to visit her in Florida. What a strange feeling it was to accept without having to get permission. At the orphanage, we had to ask permission for every little thing. Now I could fly away to Florida with no ones permission but my own. I liked this new found freedom!

Margaret and her husband, Clark, worked every day so I was on my own. After cleaning up their house, I would head for the beach. I loved the waves, the sand and the sea gulls.

One day, a man and two ladies, dressed in street clothes, approached me. They asked if I would like to enter the Miss Northwest Florida contest. I told them no as I was from Alabama and would probably not be eligible. They assured me that my address was not a consideration and further informed me that every girl who entered received a beautiful white swimsuit. The winner would receive $300.00 and a new wardrobe. That sounded great; I could certainly use a new swimsuit.

The contest was held the following Saturday. About forty five girls paraded in alike white swimsuits on a high platform built right on the beach. The newspaper reported some 10,000 spectators were in attendance.

The girl that I thought should win was a beautiful, soft spoken redhead. The girl who knew she would win was a short, bad tempered brunette named Sheila. She tried to demoralize the other contestants, even threatened them to stay out of her way. Sheila did not bother me. I laughed at her bad behavior as she reminded me of my old nemesis, Katie.

In the end, the pretty redhead did not win. Neither did Sheila. For some reason, the judges picked me. They certainly could not have selected anyone who needed the clothes and money more than I did. The following day, the Montgomery Newspaper read, Alabama Girl Steals Florida Title.

My stopping off place in Montgomery gratefully came to a close. I had my piece of paper that certified me as a licensed cosmetologist. Now I could support myself.

# FIFTY-FIVE

The campus of Samford University was everything I had imagined it would be. Tall, stately buildings mushroomed from the well-kept grounds from Lakeshore Drive all the way up the hill to the girls dormitory. I quickly unpacked my one suitcase, my one steam iron, and then took off to find Winnah.

Upon finding her, I quickly noted that she was very grown up, more beautiful and vibrant than ever. I also noticed that we hardly knew each other. She seemed more like a distant cousin than a sister. This was so disconcerting that it took me several days to come to the truth. We had not seen each other but a couple of times during the past two years. The seven years prior to that we had been together one hour per week (campus hour), outside of brief encounters at church and choir practice. We had not slept under the same roof since Mother died. That was a long time. Somehow, Winnah and I would just have to get reacquainted.

I took to campus life and dormitory living like a duckling takes to water. I was there to work and go to school so that's what I did. That was all I did! I worked 25 to 30 hours per week in a nice beauty salon, spending the rest of my time in class or studying.

I was so totally engrossed with my own goals that I was oblivious to those around me. One day, three girls who lived on my hall verbally jumped me. They demanded to know why I wasn't homesick like they were. Didn't I miss my parents, my home? I was amused, explaining to them that I had no parents and no home to be homesick for.

Returning to my room I told my roommate, Ann, that we had to think of something to help the freshman girls feel more at home, less homesick.

After church, the next day, I told Ann that we were going to the woods behind our dormitory.

"What on earth for?" she asked.

"To get a Christmas tree," I responded.

"Look," she reasoned, "we have no tool to cut down a tree. Even if we had a saw or an ax to cut it, then we would have no decorations for it."

Stubbornly I replied, "You just come with me to the woods. We will have a tree then we will have decorations!"

After church, we went to the woods finding a small pine tree, not much past a seedling. Ann held it to one side while I stomped on its small trunk. Finally cracking it, we pulled, tugged, twisted it around and around until we managed to break it from it's root. Good! Now we had a tree; next, the decorations!

Returning to our dorm, Ann and I went up and down the hall inviting everyone to our Christmas Party. We also asked for cookies, cake, or any kind of snacks the girls were willing to donate. Next, we asked them to lend us their jewelry, anything shiny or colorful. In thirty minutes our little tree was beautifully adorned with dangling earrings and garlands of beads.

Such a tree I've never seen before or since.

Ann and I hosted our first party with no food, no accommodations, nor entertainment furnished by us. However, there was plenty of food. Our guests spilled out of our tiny room, sitting on the floor of the hallway. They entertained themselves by comparing feelings of leaving home. I listened with great interest. Other than missing my brothers, I had no idea what they were talking about. Several of the girls invited me to spend the holidays with their families. I declined their invitations, citing the need to work and make money.

Soon after, an alumni of Samford University and a sorority advisor called me. She, Mrs. Rainey, invited me to join the Delta Zeta sorority.

"Thank you so much. I believe I would enjoy being a member, but I have no money for social clubs," I told her.

"I am aware of your situation; that is why I am calling you personally. I have been authorized to pay all your dues and other expenses including your pin." she explained.

"No, thank you, Mrs. Rainey; that would be charity," I declared.

"Not at all," she responded. "You will earn every dime. Just think of it as a trade. The sorority needs your maturity, your leadership, not to mention your good grades. The point average of our chapter is far below the national average. Your grades alone would help improve that average. Oh, yes, there is one other thing that you might be able to help us with. Could you help the other girls study?"

"Yes ma'am," I said. "That sounds, to me, like a good trade, and I accept. Thank you very much for asking me. I am truly honored."

So, that is how I became a sorority girl. Mother had taught me to learn all I could about everything. Social events such as parties, teas and banquets were completely foreign to me. This was my chance to learn.

In January, during my first semester final exams, I received a phenomenal letter from Mama 'daris. She stated that, although the church had been released as my clothing people, that they still wanted to help me. Elkdale Baptist Church had voted to send me $25.00 per month. Enclosed was my first check. I fell to my knees in gratitude. I knew these wonderful people sent the check for clothes, but I could do without clothes. What I really needed most was food. Earning only one dollar per hour, I had to work a lot of hours just to eat. Elkdale's check meant that I could work twenty-five fewer hours per month, and still afford to eat. The additional time would allow me to take two extra subjects per semester, thereby, graduating in three years. This had been my goal all along. "Thank you, Lord, for the wonderful people who inhabit this earth."

My grades were high enough, that the school allowed me to take two extra subjects each of the remaining semesters. These extra semester credits, plus those I would earn in summer classes would surely help me reach my goal.

My boyfriend, Tom, had been to see me several times during my first semester. He was now at the University of Alabama, working on his masters degree in civil engineering. I loved Tom. He was brilliant, witty and quite handsome. Without knowing it, Tom had taught me many things. I had never been to a restaurant, a museum, nor an opera until Tom took me. Our relationship had a good chance of becoming permanent except that Tom became impatient. "Marry me! Now or never!" he proclaimed. I was petrified. That marry word scared me to death. I mumbled something about wanting to finish school first. What I meant was: Although I had learned to trust Mr. Cox and Mr. Shirey, I still had a basic mistrust of men, in general. So I answered, "Tom, since you put it that way, I'll just have to say never."

Tom never returned. His absence left a huge void in my heart.

# FIFTY-SIX

As she did every spring and fall, Mrs. Stallworth came to Birmingham to do her spring buying for her store. As usual, she called, asking me to have dinner with her. How exciting!

In anticipation of another wonderful evening with Mrs. Stallworth, I quickly polished my one good pair of leather heels, as I thought about her last visit.

We had a wonderful time together. Never having been to a hotel before, and never having ridden an elevator, I had great memories of riding all the way to the twelfth floor of the Dinkler Tutwiler Hotel to meet her. When Mrs. Stallworth had finished dressing, she treated me to a delicious meal at an expensive restaurant called La Paree. On that occasion, I listened closely to the way Mrs. Stallworth enunciated; I mimicked the way she walked. I envied her command of waiters. I even admired the way she removed her gloves. I memorized her every move, knowing I could learn a great deal from her.

Wearing my very best dress, I caught the bus to downtown Birmingham where majestically stood the Dinkler Tutwiller Hotel.

My heart beat faster as I entered the elevator, wondering what wonderful adventure Mrs. Stallworth had planned for us.

Upon entering her room, I quickly realized that my expectations had been far too high. Mrs. Stallworth was entertaining a salesman with more than a few drinks.

Mrs. Stallworth ordered three dinners to be sent to her room. By the time the food arrived, I had lost my appetite, as she began to play the big I and little you game as soon as I entered the room. I knew I was in the wrong place.

Mrs. Stallworth excused herself to go to the ladies room. After having heard the entire history of this poor little orphan girl, the salesman seized the moment by offering me money in exchange for certain favors. I thanked him for his offer, assuring him that I did not need help.

"Well, at least let me drive you back to school," he insisted.

For self protection, I quickly countered his question with one of my own. I looked him straight in the eye and asked, "Then how would I get my car back to school?"

I stood on a dark street corner for forty-five minutes before the bus came, spending that time analyzing why such a refined lady as Mrs. Stallworth could be so hurtful. Had I thought it was intentional, the relationship would have ended a long time ago.

Learning that I could make more money per hour as a model, I gradually quit doing hair. I made it my business to know every fashion coordinator, in every department store, in Birmingham. My resume wasn't exactly a lie, but it certainly did embellish my experience. One thing that was totally truthful, however, was my dependability. This quality seemed to net more and more runway jobs. It was hard to believe that the department stores would pay such high wages for something that was so much fun.

After one of my fittings for an upcoming fashion show, I waited on the street corner for my bus back to campus. A stranger, a gray haired man of middle age, approached me, telling me he was awfully hungry and asking me to help him. I felt so sorry for this man that I gave him nearly every dime I had, holding back just enough for the bus fare.

There was a short order restaurant specializing in hot dogs on the very corner I was waiting for the bus. I sincerely thought the man would go straight to the restaurant to satisfy his hunger. Instead, he continued to pan handle every passerby on the street, telling them the same sad story he had told me. I had been taken!

I wanted to demand my money back from this man. Instead, I decided that I had a lot to learn. I would memorize his face to serve as a future reminder not to be so stupid. I would pass on the kindnesses that had been shown to me but I would certainly choose the recipient more carefully.

The consequences of my misdirected kindness meant that I had no money for food. My roommate did have a jar of peanut butter and one jar of dill pickles. After six days of eating peanut butter spread on dill pickles, I believe I learned my lesson quite well.

# FIFTY-SEVEN

It was toward the end of my second semester at Samford that I received the terrible news, the inevitable message that I long feared and dreaded. Harley had been expelled from the orphanage. The only detail of his expulsion was, that he had been given a choice of going to jail or joining the Air Force. Two days before his seventeenth birthday, Harley joined the Air Force. It was months before I knew where Harley was or what had happened to him.

As I pieced the story together, it seems that one of the town boys cornered Harley in the bathroom at school. His final verbal abuse was when he called Harley an orphan bastard. Years of pint up anger were taken out on Harley's abuser. The boy found himself in the hospital with a broken arm, bruises, and several missing teeth.

That evening, a carload of town boys came to the campus to kill Harley. Mr. McGee gave neither support, nor protection to Harley.

Armed with a baseball bat, Harley mightily defended himself, hospitalizing three more boys. In a strange way, I was proud of Harley. I, of all people, understood his rage and anger at the world. I understood his need to get even no matter the cost. In the past, I had done revengeful things, to my own detriment. I had just hoped that Harley would be past all the hurt, as I was. Venting his anger had lost Harley a very valuable college scholarship.

# FIFTY-EIGHT

Summer came; it was time for me to give up my title as Miss Northwest Florida. It would be my honor to crown the new winner.

An airplane ticket arrived in the mail. Wow! I really felt like a queen! As though my first chance to fly wasn't enough, I was informed that, before I could give up my crown, I had to act as the queen of the Billy Bowlegs Festival.

Billy Bowlegs was a legendary pirate who invaded the city of Fort Walton, eons before. Each year, the city's most eligible bachelor acted as Billy Bowlegs, invading the city, declaring a three day celebration for all the citizens. Of course, every pirate needs a lady! That was my part.

Quickly, I fashioned an outfit by cutting off the legs of a pair of pants. Short shorts, an off the shoulder blouse, and borrowed hoop earrings seemed to be appropriate for a girl who was about to be carried off by a pirate.

Although my pirate was big and strong, I felt rather sorry for him. He had to throw me over his shoulder and carry me, the wench, up the gang plank. I had finally grown to a lanky 5'8" tall and weighed 130 pounds.

Of course this was all in fun! Standing at the bow of a giant, make-believe pirate ship, I was bedazzled by the spectacle of hundreds of small boats following. I felt the wind in my hair as I thought of my Mother's words, "All of my children are special." The memory of her words and the magic of the moment made me know that she was right.

My Queen for a Weekend trip was great fun. I loved the lavish attention and my first flying experience. It was great fun but it was, after all, just fantasy. I was anxious to get back to school to experience a very real situation. Winnah and I were getting together again! When my terrific roommate graduated, Winnah agreed to share my room. She did confide, however, "It might not be for long; I'm getting married soon." I couldn't believe it. We finally had a chance to get re-acquainted and she was already talking about leaving me again.

Our short time together was good for us both. Winnah and I shared everything from clothes to toothpaste. Eventually, we shared pent-up feelings from our past, as well as plans for our futures. I could not believe that she loved a man so much that she was willing to trust the rest of her life with him. When I met Claude and gradually got acquainted, I came to a guarded understanding.

One day, Winnah told me about a contest to be held in our hometown of Troy. She thought I should enter because of the chance of winning $350.00. Winnah should have entered it herself. I think she would have won. Of course her plan was to marry Claude, so that left me to contend.

Entering the Pike County Maid of Cotton competition required a street dress, a swim suit, and an evening gown. I had no evening gown.

Winnah seemed convinced that I could win. "Let's go shopping," she said. "I have twenty-five dollars. Maybe we can find something for that."

Indeed we did! We found a beautiful gown marked way down to eleven dollars, which Winnah gladly paid. "I believe I owe you a dress," she said. So, Winnah, Claude and I drove the four hour trip to Troy.

I was truly surprised that I won because I told the judges the truth. People don't always like the truth. When they asked why I entered, I told them that I needed the money. In return for the $350, I promised to do a good job representing my county at the state competition.

After collecting my check, I threw the winning roses on the back seat of Claude's car. Claude drove Winnah and me back to school. All the way, I noticed a special oneness between the two of them. Maybe Winnah was right to marry him.

The state competition was a month away, so that gave me time to really buckle down with my schoolwork. So far, I had good grades that semester in everything except zoology. Miss Rawlings, my peculiar professor, announced that anyone who would not hold the school's six large snakes would fail the class. One of them was an eight foot boa constrictor which gave me nightmares, as I actually dreamed of it curling and tightening around my body. I told Miss Rawlings of my fear. I confessed to her that I could not, and would not, touch the snakes. She laughed, "And I thought you were a good student." In the end, my report card showed all A's with one D at the very bottom of the card. I did not give in; neither did Miss Rawlings.

Mr. Cox came all the way from Troy (at least I thought as much) to check on me and my grades. When he saw the D he quizzed, "How can this be?"

As always, I told Mr. Cox the truth, "I don't want to explain it. Let's just say that it was a matter of principle."

Mr. Cox smiled, "I don't believe you know how proud I am of you. Lots of children with your background become embroiled in self pity and bitterness. Your past adversities have made you strong." Mr. Cox studied my face, then added, "The first time I met you, so long ago, I knew you had something special, the strength to get past your terrible situation and contribute something good. I was right."

"Thank you. My mother told me not to let the bad actions of others ruin my life." This was all I could manage to say to this strange looking little man, whom I happened to adore. I wanted to say, "I love you for believing in me, for saving me from a terrible life," but somehow, I couldn't. Mr. Cox was such a formal person; it didn't seem appropriate to be informal. I wish I had. Mr. Cox died soon after of a heart attack. For a very long time, I felt as though my heart, too, had stopped. I so wished I had told him how very much I loved and appreciated him. Never again, would I love someone, and not tell them straight out.

Time quickly collided with the set date for the Miss Alabama Maid of Cotton Contest. Winnah helped me with the preparations but neither of our hearts was in it. We both loved Mr. Cox. His death still hung heavy on us. It made the idea of a contest seem frivolous and totally ridiculous. Still, I had promised my county to represent them well, so I put on my best acting face to honor my duty.

For fear of receiving pity, I locked my sorrow away, vowing to do my very best. My acting must have been believable as the judges picked me to win the state competition out of forty-nine counties. I gratefully accepted the large check, promptly donating it to the Samford Chapel Fund. The money was almost enough to purchase a pew with a gold plaque that simply stated, In Memory of Dr. E. E. Cox. It should have read volumes.

# FIFTY-NINE

Part of my duty as the Alabama Maid of Cotton was to travel to different states, giving speeches on behalf of the Cotton Council. I really enjoyed this, especially the flying. Cotton really was my favorite fabric, and I was more than happy to say so. As I became a more experienced speaker, I humorously told of planting, thinning, chopping and picking cotton.

Mid December came around so fast! I was in the middle of finishing up tests and shopping for the approaching National Maid of Cotton Contest when Miss Stallworth called.

I really cared about this lady; there was no way I could tell her that it was an inconvenient time for dinner.

That Friday was a full day. I was barraged with five hours of tough tests, then caught a bus to downtown Birmingham. There I met my chaperone and traveling companion to complete my wardrobe for nationals. Money was no object. My sponsors gladly paid the bill for me to have the finest dresses and gowns in Birmingham. Thank goodness Mama 'daris had taught me how to shop or my fairy tale shopping spree would have been disastrous.

My shopping list was all filled; there was just enough time to walk the seven blocks to meet Mrs. Stallworth for dinner. My feet never felt the pavement! I could hardly wait to show her my selections and get her approval.

Mrs. Stallworth opened the door to her hotel room. Standing before me was a person I had never before seen, an ugly drunk!

"You're six minutes late," Mrs. Stallworth accused in a guttural fashion. "Who do you think you are that you should treat me this way!"

"I'm sorry Mrs. Stall - - -"

"Don't tell me you're sorry. I know you're sorry trash! I suppose all these contests you've won . . . all the crowns. . and now, I hear you're on television with Bear Bryant! Guess all this makes you feel important. Well, you're not!" she yelled. "You're nothing but **poor orphan trash**! Don't you know your place? Girls with refinement and culture should be doing these things. My daughter was in line to be a Delta Zeta. Now you are!" she screamed. "My daughter could have done everything you're doing if she hadn't run off and gotten herself pregnant! Did you think you could take her place?"

I was bewildered. This was the first time Mrs. Stallworth had mentioned that she had a daughter.

For years, I truly believed that Mrs. Stallworth loved me, thinking of me as her daughter. Now, the ugly truth fell on me like a ton of rocks. Mrs. Stallworth's true feeling for me was that of hate. She despised me because I was everything that her daughter was not. Turning to leave the room, I said, "Since you have such an outstanding daughter, I'm sure you will have no further need of me."

From the hotel lobby, I called Winnah, the one person in the world I knew I could count on. One of her friends had a car and was more than glad to help rescue me.

The episode with Mrs. Stallworth hurt me so badly that I cried for two days. I knew that I had to resolve it with her when she was sober. When she verbally attacked me, Mrs. Stallworth was too drunk to realize that she had lost something mighty precious; something that would have warmed her heart into her old age. A true and loving daughter, no matter her birth, is more valuable than gold. I needed her to know that she had lost me forever.

"Maybe you should write her a letter; would that help?" Winnah suggested.

"No, I need to tell her in person that I am through with her!" I answered.

My heart still grieved, until a week later, when Mrs. Stallworth came to one of my fashion shows. After the finale, she met me at the dressing room door, arms outreached. I looked at her with a blank face. "Do we know each other?" I asked. Then, more firmly, I said to her, "I don't believe we've met," as I walked away.

That was the end of a deceptive, hateful relationship. Never again would I allow her, or anyone else, to trample upon my heart.

# SIXTY

In grand style, my sponsors sent me to Memphis, Tennessee for the National Maid of Cotton Competition. They really expected that I would win, especially since the National Press Association had picked me as most photogenic. I hated to sound negative but I seemed to know something that my sponsors didn't. They didn't seem to understand that there is no such thing as the best girl, a sure winner. Beauty, (as well as all of the other attributes upon which we were being judged such as style, personality and speaking ability), is in the eyes of the beholder. Five judges might pick one girl to win, while five different judges would select an entirely different winner.

It made me nervous that my sponsors expected so much of me. All I could do was my very best. That was all.

The week long competition got underway. There was such a bevy of beautiful girls, I felt honored just to be among them. I knew that I had one chance out of fifty-two and that was okay.

During the week, it was made clear that the winner would travel the globe, promoting cotton. I would love to do this. I could handle it! But so could every girl there, especially Miss North Carolina. Had I been one of the judges, I would have picked her.

On Friday, I received a good luck telegram from the orphanage. The names of over two hundred children were plainly spelled out. It was probably the longest telegram in history. A sense of pride and duty overwhelmed me. I knew that, if I should win, it would be like they were winners too. Now, I wanted to win more than ever. The telegram was still in my hand when I was called in for a special session with the judges. "This might be a good sign," I thought.

The head judge was very formal as he began to speak. "You might not know this, Miss Nelson, but the National Maid of Cotton comes under the highest scrutiny. So does her family. Often, her family travels with her. They have to be beyond reproach. We've debated what to do about you. We've decided to tell you that you can't win since you have no family."

I rose from my seat and handed him my telegram. "Yes, sir, I have a family. Here are all their names." There was a long silence. "Sir, I wish you hadn't told me. Not winning is okay, but losing because I am different, is very hurtful."

I left the room with no small amount of anger. For the first time in my life, I felt like an orphan.

I never told anyone about this experience. The judges, I believed, had no intentions of being mean. It was as though they felt a need to explain or apologize to me. Why? I wasn't different; I was just me . . . my mother's daughter!

At the end of the semester, Winnah married Claude. They started their lives together in New Orleans where Claude entered the seminary. I knew Claude was a wonderful man; I was glad she found him. It just seemed like Winnah and I were always being separated. New Orleans seemed like a million miles away.

Between my many jobs and taking extra classes, there was little time for social activities. That was, until I met John. I was so drawn to him that I made time to see him.

Could this be love? I didn't know. I just knew that the very thought of him made my toes curl. Mysterious, dark eyes, black hair and a perfect physique, gave John the appearance of the perfect male specimen. The fact that John was from a socially prominent, old-money family certainly did not detract from his appeal.

John was not shy about letting me know of his intentions. "I know you don't want to hear this right now, but someday, you will marry me."

Since John was so sure, I decided to take him to Selma. If he could pass the Madaris test, then I might consider his offer.

As soon as John stopped the car in front of Mama 'daris's house, he exclaimed, "My God! These folks are poor. What do they do for a living?"

John did not have to pass the Madaris test; he had just flunked mine. I wanted nothing to do with a man who judged others by the size of their house. The Madaris family had far less money than John's family, but they were richer by far.

# SIXTY-ONE

A shocking, unexpected letter was delivered to me on my birthday. It was from the Veterans Administration. It clearly stated that my father was old, ill, and needed help.

My father? I was stunned! This letter had to be a mistake. My daddy was so mean that surely someone had killed him years ago! In my heart he was dead! I had not seen nor heard from him since that terrible day he abused me on the kitchen table.

The letter was so upsetting that I had to read it several times before I could equate the full gist of it. It seems that a man, who was supposedly my father, was temporarily in the V.A. Hospital in Birmingham.

The Veterans Administration wanted to transfer him to Tuscaloosa, a special hospital for alcoholics and the mentally imbalanced. Not only did they require the permission of a relative, but it was also a matter of finance. Being a veteran of World War One, he was qualified for free treatment but only if a relative agreed to act as personal representative or guardian.

I hated for someone to need help and not be able to get it. Just the same, the Veterans Administration had asked the wrong one. Why me? I never again wanted to see or hear from this man. He did not exist!

The letter brought back memories and feelings that I thought were discarded years ago. Every night, I experienced terrible nightmares of hunger, beatings, and sexual abuse.

After a week of re-living the horror, I took a bus to downtown Birmingham to the Veterans Administration's office. I explained to the nice interviewer that I did not know this man, that we were related only by an accident of birth. I suggested that they contact one of his many brothers or sisters.

I was informed that the living brothers and sisters had already been contacted; they had refused to help!

I felt like a cornered animal! What should I do? Maybe I could push this duty off on Winnah. Being the oldest, they probably would have contacted her anyway, if they had known her new name and address.

Without thinking, I heard the question come from my mouth, "Is it just a matter of signing my name?"

The interviewer looked pleased, "Well, not exactly," he responded. "You would receive thirty-three dollars per month. It would be your duty to spend this money on your father's personal needs, such as razor blades, shampoo, etc. You would have to stay in contact with him to know his needs."

So that was it! He wanted me to become my daddy's keeper. I sat silent and dumfounded.

"I believe you will do this, otherwise why did you come?" the interviewer added.

"I'll let you know," I mumbled, as I rose to my feet.

"There is a benefit that I haven't mentioned. I believe that you have a brother, Billy, who is under eighteen years of age? If you do this, he will receive Social Security benefits."

The emotions of the interview were washed away as my good sense returned. "Could these benefits be applied to college tuition?" I asked.

"Certainly," my interviewer confirmed.

I left the building more confused than ever. Why wasn't Billy already receiving benefits? One thing I knew for sure, Billy deserved a chance to get a college education. I had no idea if he had a chance to win a scholarship.

Back at the dormitory my nightmares continued. I knew I had to do something to unburden myself of these endless dreams. That was when I concocted a fail proof plan.

I knew that some of my classmates visited the VA Hospital every Sunday afternoon. They volunteered their time to talk, visit, or read Bible stories to the men. That Sunday, the group had a new volunteer. The fact that I requested third floor was unquestioned.

I was certain that I could check out the situation without ever being recognized. I stepped off the elevator with my Bible tucked under my arm, confident that my anonymity would keep me safe, even if Daddy had gone crazy.

To my surprise and utter fear, an old guy in a wheelchair started waving and motioning for me to come to him. I did so as he wheeled his chair around, motioning me to follow. This man was so old! Was he really my daddy?

I knew his true identity as soon as we reached his room. He fumbled under his pillow pulling out newspaper clippings, all of me. He touched his chest, then pointed at me, as he handed them to me. I wanted to scream at him, "You have no claim on me! I am not your daughter." I said nothing.

Crazy or not, he communicated quite well. Lifting the knitted cover from his throat, he pointed to a large, open hole. Then he pointed to his mouth and shook his head as if to say, "I can't talk."

I felt faint! Gathering my wits and my courage, I spoke for the first time. "The VA wants to put you in the Tuscaloosa hospital. Is that okay with you?"

He nodded "yes" with a smile of appreciation that I felt was saying "I'm glad that you care about me." He was sadly mistaken.

Not wanting him to know how uncomfortable I was with the situation, I stayed for awhile, allowing him to show me around his ward. After a polite amount of time passed, I excused myself, pretending I needed to be somewhere.

With knees knocking, I left the hospital knowing that I would help him, not because he deserved it, not because I was his daughter; but because he was a pitiful old man who could not speak for himself. There was a time I could not speak for myself.

It would be dishonest to say that my helping him was a completely virtuous act. The fact that he was helpless was secondary in making my decision.

I agreed to take on this responsibility primarily because I felt that, at least one of his children should benefit from the misfortune of being born to him. Social Security benefits would now be sent to the orphanage every month. I never knew the dollar amount but I was confident that every penny would be saved for Billy's college tuition.

# SIXTY-TWO

Being the fall of the year, one of my many jobs was on Sunday afternoon. I did the television commercials for Coca-Cola and Golden Flake Potato Chips, who sponsored the live Bear Bryant Football Review. This was an honor for me as I knew Bear Bryant to be a great coach as well as a fine man.

This particular Sunday, I caught a bus back from the TV station as I often did. When I arrived at my dormitory, there were at least five messages from Elaine a member of my Sunday school class. Each message read the same, "Urgent, please call immediately."

So I called. "Elaine, what is so urgent?"

"Well, the strangest thing happened after church today. You remember talking to me?" she asked. Elaine had a habit of digressing.

"Well, of course I do. What's so urgent?" I asked.

"That's what I'm trying to tell you. As soon as you walked away this morning, this big, tall, gorgeous man walked right up to me. He said, "The girl you just spoke to is the girl I'm going to marry, if she's still single, and her name is not Mildred."

"Who was this girl?" I asked.

"Well, it was you, of course," Elaine clarified.

"What did you tell him?" I asked.

"Well, I was so surprised at his statement that I'm not sure what I said. I think I laughed as I asked, how did you know?"

"Know what? That's she's married?" he prompted.

"No, that her name is Mildred!"

"You should have seen his face! Just the same, he still wanted to know how to call you. I hope you don't mind, but I told him you lived on campus at Samford."

"Well . . ."

"By the way, his name is Jim Holmes."

"I remember seeing a man who seemed really familiar to me but I know we've never met. Does he have sandy blonde hair and a boyish smile?" I quizzed.

"Yes. And he was really tall. Let me know if he calls."

"I don't believe he will bother to find my number; not if he hates my name," I told Elaine.

Jim Holmes did call and secretly, it pleased me. It also confused me. My mistrust of men, especially one that mentioned marriage without having met me, caused my protective guard to go way up.

I pretended little interest in meeting him, not letting him know that I had noticed him. I informed him that I was unaccustomed to going out on blind dates. Then I waited to see if this guy had enough self confidence to sway me.

Sway? What followed was probably the finest sales pitch I had ever heard before or since. He sold me on going out with him the following Friday night. I further tested his resolve.

"I have a sorority meeting scheduled for late Friday afternoon; I have no idea when it will be over. Would you mind waiting for me in the lobby until it is over?" I asked.

"Sure, I'll meet you there," he agreed.

As I hung up the phone I couldn't help admiring this fellow. I gave him a hard time but he never backed off. Most guys would have. I needed to know what he was made of . . . and I liked the results. Self confidence and determination were two of the qualities I greatly admired. Come Friday, I would find out about some of his other qualities.

That Friday, I admit to speeding up the meeting; I was looking forward to going out with this Jim Holmes. As planned, Jim was waiting for me in the lobby. "Good, you're not late, but we do need to hurry," he stated as he whisked me out the door.

We drove directly to the Civic Center as he told me we would. On the way, Jim told me about his job as a detail man (pharmaceutical salesman) for Pfizer Laboratories. Pfizer was hosting a banquet with live entertainment for the Medical Association members and spouses.

Upon arrival, Jim introduced me to a couple of doctors and their wives. He seated me before a beautiful steak dinner, then said, "I've got to get backstage; I'm part of the show."

Part of the show? Jim was the main event. Dressed in a plaid suit with pant legs about four inches too short, he, mimicking a country bumpkin, played a wide variety of musical instruments. I loved his music as well as his comedy routine. I couldn't remember ever laughing so much. This definitely did not feel like a first date. By evenings end I was smitten with this overgrown Georgia boy.

Uh, oh - that protective guard was being lowered. I had best watch myself. This man could hurt me. I knew it, but there was no way I would let him know it.

On returning to the dormitory, twenty or more girls mobbed me as I entered the hall. "Who is he?" they demanded.

"It's just Jim Holmes," I informed them in a detached fashion. I had learned long ago not to show my true feelings.

One of my hall-mates, Katie, said, "He's not just Jim Holmes; he's the Britling Man! We have lunch every Sunday at Britling's just to see him."

"Have any of you ever tried to meet him?" I asked.

Almost in unison they said, "No."

"Well, if I liked someone that much, I would find a way to meet him," I told them. "I'll be glad to introduce you, if you like. I don't really have time for a boyfriend."

So that was the beginning of my introducing Jim to my friends, one at a time. He asked none of them out.

"Are you trying to get rid of me? If not, why are you introducing me to all your friends?" Jim asked.

"Well, I suppose a man has to date a lot of different girls to know what he likes best," I reasoned.

"I already know what and who I like best and it is you! I know that you like me too. Now, would you please just cut out the antics?" he demanded.

I looked hard at Jim, recognizing him as a man of serious intent. Boy, was he smart! He was on to me and stated it plainly. I liked his intuitiveness.

Jim was relentless in his pursuit of me. While I strongly resisted his steady, sure knowing that we were meant for each other. I insisted that he had his sights on the wrong girl, that we could be friends only.

"Okay, if that's the way you want it," he said.

But, he seemed to call and take me out more often than before.

The truth is, I really liked being with Jim. Had he stopped calling, I would have been lost. Sometimes we went to a movie or dinner, but more often we went for long walks on the nature trail, as we shared an interest in plants and wildlife.

Once, when I had a cold, Jim sent me a polished red apple, covered with candy kisses that he fastened with toothpicks. Many Sunday afternoons were spent on a high bluff overlooking all of south Birmingham. There we shared a part of our past, our hopes and dreams for the future. I was so comfortable with Jim; I could tell him anything.

As a means of self-protection, I had learned to be on guard, to never show my real self, my innermost thoughts and feelings to anyone, especially not a male. The need to protect myself ceased to exist when I was with him. Jim seemed to enjoy talking and sharing ideas with me. He confided that he had stopped dating my friend, Susan, who was Alabama's Miss Universe at the time.

"She is beautiful but boring," he admitted. "The only subject she has an opinion about is dieting. I'm not interested in dieting, and I've never heard you mention the word."

Having Jim as my best friend was very convenient. When he wasn't working, he was more than happy to drive me to my various jobs, including live television commercials and fashion shows. Most of the time, he just stayed and watched the show.

Having Jim as my best friend was sometimes embarrassing. He frequently showed up at my sports competitions. When the game was over, he walked me back to my dormitory. That was the embarrassing part. I hated for him to see me all sweaty and smelling like a mule. Besides, athletic girls were not well thought of in the early sixties. The more popular girls were delicate and non-aggressive.

One day, after a fight-to-the-end volleyball game, Jim walked me to my dorm as usual. On the way he surmised, "With your competitive nature and my size, we could have some terrific children, maybe professional athletes."

"I thought we had agreed not to talk about marriage," I reminded. In my heart I was glad to know that he liked my tomboyish ways. He appreciated my sweaty efforts to win a volleyball game just as much as he admired my prancing down the runway in beautiful, expensive gowns.

"I said nothing about marriage," Jim grinned.

"Well, I surely would not want children without marriage," I answered.

Slowly, I developed a deep caring for Jim which should have been a good thing. Instead, it was the most frightening experience of my life. I was afraid to care so much, to commit myself to another person. Besides, he just didn't fit in with my plans. In record time, I was about to finish all my required courses at Samford University. Afterwards, I had a scholarship waiting for me in New York. How could our friendship exist with us so far apart?

After discussing with Jim, my plans to go to New York, he calmly responded, "You go on and do what you need to do. When the time is right, you will know that we belong together. I will wait for that time."

What patience! I had never known anyone with such single-minded determination! Was this deep feeling between us called love? I didn't know, but as graduation day neared, the trappings of New York began to lose their appeal. I knew in my heart that Jim was my forever and always sweetheart and that I could not bear to leave him.

My decision to marry Jim was based on a deep trust that I had longed for without knowing it. I knew he would never walk heavy on my heart, already fragile from childhood wear.

Jim's heart was rich but his wallet was almost as thin as mine. When he suggested that we shop for an engagement ring, I told him I didn't want one.

"Are you embarrassed to show everyone that you are engaged to me?" Jim asked.

I knew I would never hide anything from Jim, so I told him the honest truth. "No, it's just that I know you don't have a lot of money. There is something else I would much rather have."

"What could be more important than an engagement ring?" he asked.

"A home; my very own house is what I want." I stated.

Jim looked worried. "I'm not sure we can do that," he said.

"Sure we can; I have saved $300.00 whole dollars. I can hold back one hundred for our wedding and put two hundred down on our house. Let's go house shopping!"

Jim laughed with amusement.

Jim was twenty-seven years old and familiar with finance and such. I was twenty with no experience in such things as down payments and finance dealings. Jim might have laughed at my innocence, but he didn't. He laughed in appreciation for my optimistic attitude.

After looking at several locations and houses we happened on a new development with thirty or more houses, all vacant, most half built. The smallest one, a beautiful three bedroom, two bath, brick rancher was built on the perfect lot. I knew it had to be ours so we hunted up the builder with a proposition.

The builder, Mr. Flemming, laughingly said, "The down payment is a few thousand, not two hundred dollars."

I was undaunted. "If someone was living in this house, it might help the others to sell. Besides, I am near graduation and by January, I will have a full-time job; I will pay you every dime I make until the down payment is satisfied."

Mr. Flemming, eyeing me, closely, asked, "Do you know what a closing is?"

"No, sir," I answered.

"Well, basically it means that all the money you give me could be a loss to you if the bank does not agree to finance you. Anyway, you're just engaged; what if you get disengaged?" he asked thoughtfully.

I could see he was giving in so I quickly wrote a check. Handing it to him, I answered, "then you get to keep my two hundred dollars."

Looking at the check, Mr. Flemming reasoned, "then you do understand about earnest money?"

"No sir; I just know this is my house," I smilingly replied.

I don't believe the builder was being generous. Having nothing to lose, he acted on impulse, persuaded by a young woman's great desire for her own home. I knew and he knew that our verbal contract would be honored.

Jim moved into our new home where I would soon join him, after our wedding. During the move, we spontaneously curled up on the hardwood floor in the middle of our vacant living room. I confessed to him that, except for my childhood abuse, I was a virgin. I also confided that I was afraid of sex.

"You have no reason to be afraid; I will never hurt you. Sex happens naturally and wonderfully between two people who love each other. I have been waiting for you to love me that much."

Jim held me for a long time before he spoke again.

"I think you hypnotized that builder," he grinned. Delayed closings are unheard of. We should have our down payment finished and closed out by next June. That's about the same time your brother Billy will be graduating and leaving the orphanage. Why don't we invite him to live with us while he goes to college?"

My love for Jim quickly multiplied as I realized his concern and kindness towards my brother whom he had never met. All my small doubts about getting married were washed away. Jim was a good, loving man, the person I wanted to be with from now to forever. I could hardly wait until December the sixteenth, the beginning of my whole life, my wedding day.

# SIXTY-THREE

The busiest time of my life was interrupted by a small, blue envelope that came in the mail. The return address read: Betty Coons, Fayette, Alabama

I immediately recognized her name, quickly opening the envelope. The letter read:

Dear Mildred,

I am so happy that things have evidently turned out so well for you. I have followed your achievements through the newspaper, TV, and various other sources. Last month, I read where you had been selected for "Who's Who in American Schools and Colleges."

Each time I learned of some new honor, I planned to sit down and write you to tell you how happy and proud I was.

Today, when I read of your engagement, I decided it was time to do more than have good intentions.

I suppose I should explain who I am. I am sure you must be puzzled as it has been quite a few years since you knew me and probably you were too young to remember me.

I was the social worker who, after your mother's death, took you and placed you, Winnah, Harley, and Billy in the orphanage. At the time, I prayed that I was doing the right thing. A case worker can never look far ahead enough to know what is best.

I hope you feel that going to the orphanage was for the best since it was your life that was affected by my decision.

I hope things have turned out well for Winnah. I remember how unhappy she was and very sad about being separated from your baby sister and brother. She cried most of the way to Troy.

What has happened to Harley and Billy? Are they still at the Home?

I would like to extend to you all my best wishes for your forthcoming marriage. I am sure you will have all the happiness you so richly deserve.

Sincerely,

Betty Coons

I gathered together all the coins I could find or borrow and headed for the pay phone on our hall. Upon getting connected with Miss Coons, I identified myself, then thanked her for what she had done for me, my brothers and sister.

Nothing but silence came from the other end of the line.

"Are you there?" I asked.

"Yes," Miss Coons replied. "It's just that I am so surprised. I've never had a child I helped to call me."

"Maybe they don't remember you, but I do," I stated.

"Was the orphanage a wonderful place to grow up?" Miss Coons asked.

"No, ma'am, I wouldn't say it was wonderful, but it was okay . . . a far better place than where we came from. That's why I called you. I'm just so grateful that you took us away from our grandparents. I cringe when I think of how our lives would have been had it not been for you."

"Do you really mean that?" she asked.

"Yes, I do, and furthermore I am convinced that orphanages fulfill a definite need in our society. Orphanages may generally have negative reputations, but my experiences were mostly positive."

The voice of Miss Coons took on a very firm, knowing sound. "The Lord works in mysterious ways; you have just made a decision for me. I have been agonizing for weeks over what to do about two little boys. Now I know what to do."

As I hung up the phone, I felt a deep gratitude, something approaching reverence for a woman that I hardly knew, a woman whose conscientious attention to her job resulted in such positive results for all four of us.

# SIXTY -FOUR

The December wedding between Jim and me appeared to have cost thousands of dollars. My actual cost was $84.00, as practically everything was borrowed or donated. Who was to know that my exquisite gown with a long, flowing train had been recently worn by one of my good friends! I was honored to wear it. From the woods came lush greenery to decorate the church. A good friend allowed me to strip his camellia bushes of all it's beautiful, red blooms with waxy, green leaves.

The Madaris family was wonderful; they used their multiple talents to help me. James, a printer, made our invitations. Evelyn hosted our after-rehearsal party. Daisy handmade a lovely peignoir set for me. Charles Junior arranged for all of Jim's family to have a cost free place to stay on the army base. Mama 'daris and several of her daughters saved and froze juice from canned fruit. The juice was later thawed and mixed with Seven-up for serving from my borrowed punch bowl. The red camellias looked great against the stark, white table cloths.

Of course, use of the church was also a donation of the Elkdale Baptist Church congregation, who had recently built a large, new sanctuary. Having the ceremony at Elkdale was my way of saying "thank you" to all its wonderful members who had helped me over the years.

Walking down the aisle, I subconsciously reviewed my entire life.

I thought of my beautiful mother; how I wished she could be here this day.

I felt a deep sense of gratitude for my years at the Alabama Baptist Children's Home, for its safety and opportunities to better myself.

Remembering the first time meeting Mr. Cox, I recollected his steady, sure guidance that had helped me to find a whole new path.

My childhood abusers flashed throughout my mind. They had actually strengthened me.

My life was totally unimaginable without my terrific Madaris family. They had helped me in ways they were totally unaware.

Escorting me down the isle, Mr. Shirey, my stand-in Dad, beamed with pleasure. I smiled at him and squeezed his arm - my way of saying, "You mean so much to me. You taught me how to appreciate and enjoy life. You taught my heart to sing."

I thought of God's grace, for His saving me from a terrible life. "Thank you, God, for taking away the pain, the hate, freeing my heart to love."

Nearing the altar, I could see Jim's smiling face and reaching arms. I knew he would never harm me, nor would I harm him. From now on, life would be filled with love and happiness.

My total concentration should have been on the ceremony. This was my special day. I wanted to savor and remember every second of it. For some reason, I found it difficult, if not impossible, to concentrate on the present. As I read Jim's face, my mind's eye jumped far into the future.

To myself, I took this solemn oath; "Never again will my life be about hurt. Moreover, neither past hurts nor a bad childhood will rule my life or be used by me as an excuse when I, (as all human beings inevitably do), experience failures and disappointments."

I smiled at the minister, not hearing a word he said. Jim took my hand and recited his vows to me perfectly, without prompting from the minister. I tried really hard to focus on what Jim was saying, but the love that shown through his eyes overshadowed his words.

Then came my turn to say my vows. Some out of body experience must have engulfed me. I mechanically repeated back to Jim exactly what he had said to me, changing only the name. Jim had properly taken me to be his wife; but I had, unknowingly, also taken him to be my wife. Jim, in an attempt to correct me, squeezed my hand and whispered "husband." I had no idea of what I had said or why he again prompted, "husband." I just continued my recitation. My mind was apparently elsewhere, absorbed in visions of our future together.

As I felt our hearts completely join, a sudden vision of two old people came to mind.

"Yes," I imagined, "when we are old and gray, Jim and I will erect a toy train track with electric trains running against the walls and meandering through every room in the house. There will be a single seated swing, attached to high rafters, decorated with colorful ribbons that peacefully float behind me as I swing. When visitors come to our house, they will say, "Look at those old folks! They are in their second childhood!" With a wink at Jim and a half smile, I will say, "No. . . First."

# EPILOGUE

Over forty years have gone by since this story ended. Only five of Mother's nine children survive. The author and two of her brothers, Billy and Sam are college graduates. All five have attended a college or university. All have become stable adults with no predisposition to passing on to their children, or anyone else, the abuse they suffered as children. Winnah and her husband, a Baptist minister, have devoted their lives to caring for underprivileged and abused children. Each of our homes has been a refuge for distressed children in need on many occasions.

If the scars of the past have left any bitterness in any of us, it certainly is not apparent. This is a fun loving bunch. As a matter of fact, they are a loving bunch. July 4th and Thanksgiving are two special days for us, as these are the times of year that we get together for a reunion. Thanksgiving is usually a four to five day affair filled with card playing, games, jam sessions, song, the banter of teen agers and the laughter of little children.

The author's home is filled with wall-to-wall people - three generations of happy, well adjusted grandparents, parents and grandchildren.

This tradition is now being replicated by another generation.

It is my wish that these celebrations will continue. I believe they will.

Life is good!

# A FINAL WORD

If you are one of those unfortunate individuals who has experienced abuse as a child, I have this tried and true advice.

Do not listen to those over-used, vulgar cliches such as, "Get over it" or "Move on." This approach is ludicrous.

You don't even have to try to forget the unpleasantness of the past. Every good thing and every bad thing that has happened to us in the past has combined to make us what we are today. We can accept the past and from the acknowledgment of it gain strength and control our own destiny, or we can dwell upon it, feel sorry for ourselves and let those who have harmed us control our destiny. Dwelling on someone's hateful actions gives them power over you. It will also turn you into a whining, bitter person.

Don't ever let your bitterness become an excuse for acting out upon others the horrible deeds that were done to you. Be thankful that you survived, and fortunate that the experience has made you a stronger person.

In short.. You can hate a person's conduct without hating the person. If you hate the conduct, you're not likely to replicate it yourself. If you hate a person; however, that hate will fester inside and, like a cancer, will eventually consume you.